Hymns of Praise for All Keyboards.

Wise Publications
London/New York/Paris/Sydney/Copenhagen/Madrid

Exclusive Distributors:
Music Sales Limited
8/9 Frith Street, London W1V 5TZ, England.
Music Sales Pty Limited
120 Rothschild Avenue, Rosebery, NSW 2018, Australia.

Order No. AM91082
ISBN 0-7119-3413-4
This book © Copyright 1993 by Wise Publications

Designed by Studio Twenty, London
Music arranged by Daniel Scott
Music processed by Seton Music Graphics

Printed in the United Kingdom by
Redwood Books Limited, Trowbridge, Wiltshire.

Your Guarantee of Quality
As publishers, we strive to produce every book to the
highest commercial standards.
The music has been freshly engraved and the book has
been carefully designed to minimise awkward page turns and
to make playing from it a real pleasure.
Particular care has been given to specifying acid-free, neutral-sized
paper made from pulps which have not been elemental chlorine
bleached. This pulp is from farmed sustainable forests
and was produced with special regard for the environment.
Throughout, the printing and binding have been planned to
ensure a sturdy, attractive publication which should give years of
enjoyment. If your copy fails to meet our high standards, please
inform us and we will gladly replace it.

Music Sales' complete catalogue lists thousands of titles and is
free from your local music shop, or direct from Music Sales Limited.
Please send a cheque/postal order for £1.50 for postage to:
Music Sales Limited, Newmarket Road, Bury St. Edmunds,
Suffolk IP33 3YB.

Christ, Whose Glory Fills The Skies

Music: Melody from J.G. Werner's *Choralbuch*, Leipzig, 1815,
arr. W.H. Havergal (1793-1870)
Words: Charles Wesley (1707 -1788)

Suggested registration: Organ   Rhythm: 8 beat

2. Dark and cheerless is the morn
   Unaccompanied by Thee;
   Joyless is the day's return,
   Till Thy mercy's beams I see;
   Till they inward light impart,
   Glad my eyes, and warm my heart.

3. Visit then this soul of mine;
   Pierce the gloom of sin and grief;
   Fill me, radiancy divine;
   Scatter all my unbelief;
   More and more Thyself display,
   Shining to the perfect day.

All Glory, Laud, And Honour

Music: Melchior Teschner (c.1615),
Harmony from J.S. Bach (1685-1750)
Words: Theodulph of Orleans (c.750-821) tr. J.M. Neale (1818-1866)

Suggested registration: Organ   Rhythm: Rock

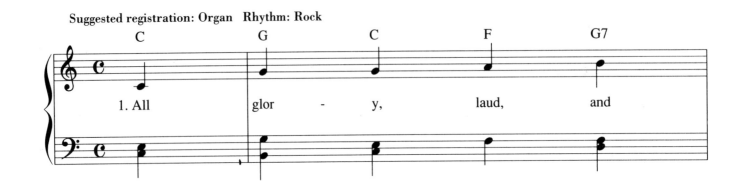

1. All glor - y, laud, and

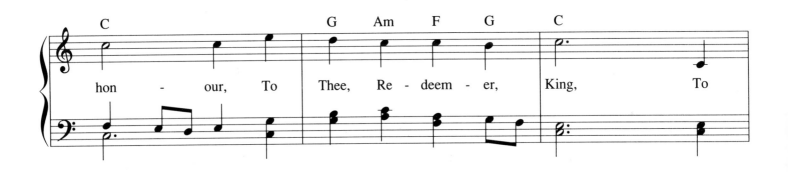

hon - our, To Thee, Re - deem - er, King, To

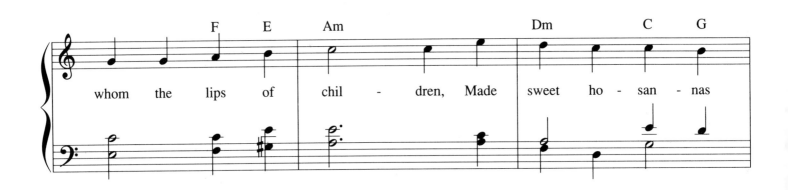

whom the lips of chil - dren, Made sweet ho - san - nas

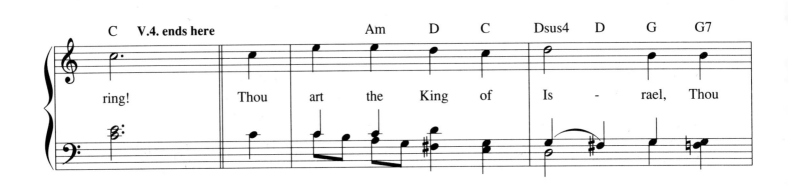

ring! Thou art the King of Is - rael, Thou

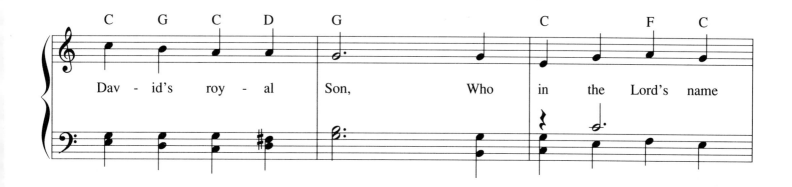

Dav - id's roy - al Son, Who in the Lord's name

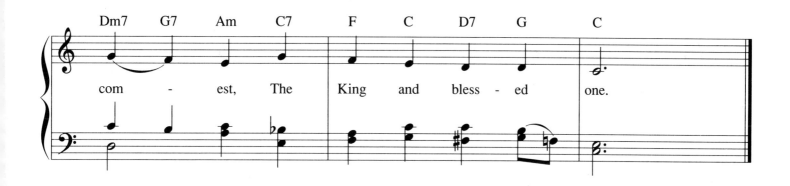

com - est, The King and bless - ed one.

2. The company of angels
   Are praising Thee on high,
   And mortal men and all things
   Created make reply.
   The people of the Hebrews
   With palms before Thee went;
   Our praise and prayer and anthems
   Before Thee we present.

3. To Thee before Thy passion
   They sang their hymns of praise;
   To the now high exalted
   Our melody we raise.
   Thou didst accept their praises;
   Accept the prayers we bring,
   Who in all good delightest,
   Thou good and gracious King.

4. All glory, laud, and honour
   To Thee, Redeemer, King,
   To whom the lips of children
   Made sweet hosannas sing!

All Things Bright And Beautiful

Music: W.H. Monk (1823-1889)
Words: Cecil F. Alexander (1818-1895)

Suggested registration: Piano   Rhythm: 8 beat

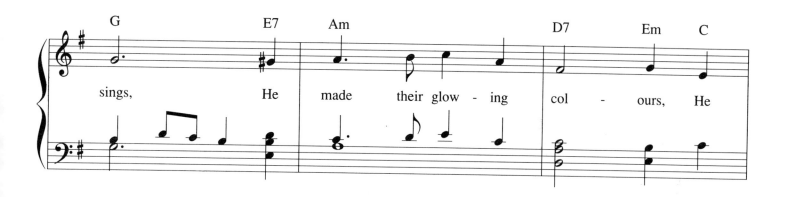

sings,   He   made   their glow - ing   col -   ours,   He

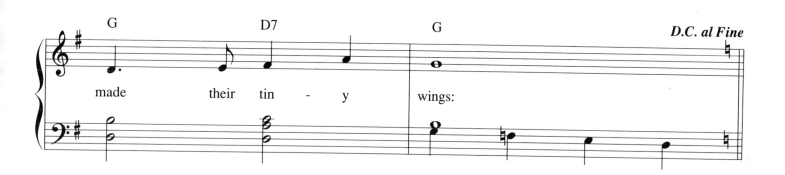

D.C. al Fine

made   their   tin -   y   wings:

Refrain

2. The purple-headed mountain,
   The river running by,
   The sunset, and the morning
   That brightens up the sky:

Refrain

3. The cold wind in the winter,
   The pleasant summer sun,
   The ripe fruits in the garden,
   He made them every one:

Refrain

4. He gave us eyes to see them,
   And lips that we might tell
   How great is God Almighty,
   Who has made all things well:

Refrain

Amazing Grace

Music: Traditional
and arranged Roland Fudge
Words: John Newton (1725-1807)

Suggested registration: Harp   Rhythm: Waltz

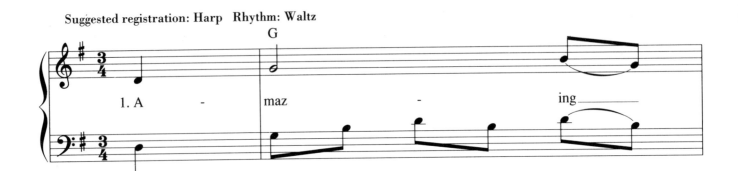

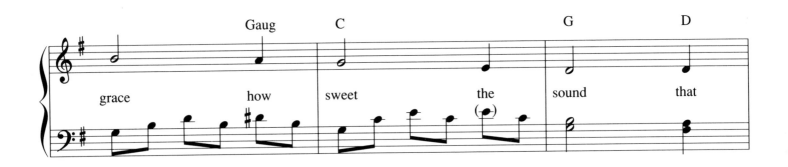

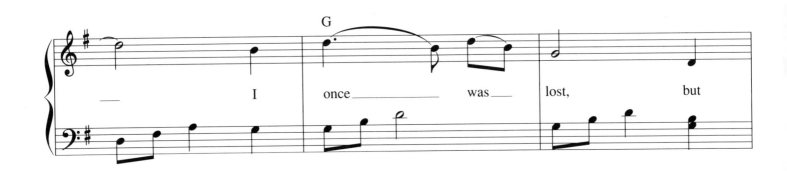

now _____ am ___ found, Was blind, but ___

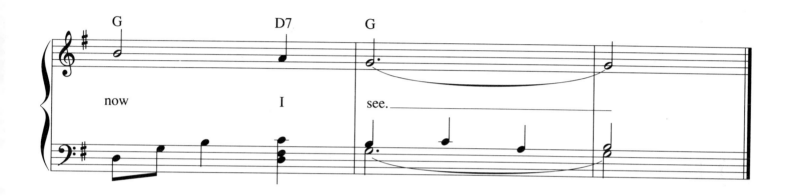

now I see. _____

2. Through many dangers, toils and snares
   I have already come;
   God's grace has brought me safe thus far,
   And he will lead me home.

3. The Lord has promised good to me,
   His word my hope secures;
   He will my shield and portion be
   As long as life endures.

4. And, when this heart and flesh shall fail
   And mortal life shall cease,
   I shall possess within the veil
   A life of joy and peace.

Blessed Assurance

Music: Mrs J. F. Knapp (1839-1908)
Words: Frances van Alstyne (1820-1915)

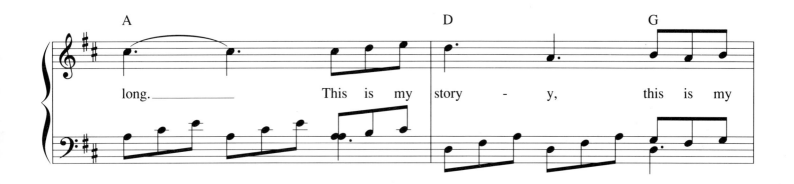

long._____ This is my story - y, this is my

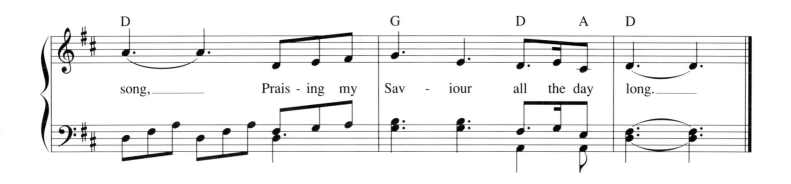

song,_____ Prais - ing my Sav - iour all the day long._____

2. Perfect submission, perfect delight,
   Visions of rapture burst on my sight;
   Angels descending bring from above
   Echoes of mercy, whispers of love:

   Refrain

3. Perfect submission, all is at rest,
   I in my Saviour am happy and blessed;
   Watching and waiting, looking above,
   Filled with his goodness, lost in his love:

   Refrain

Come Let Us Join Our Cheerful Songs

Music: Henry Lahee (1826-1912)
Words: Isaac Watts (1674-1748)

Suggested registration: Organ   Rhythm: Disco

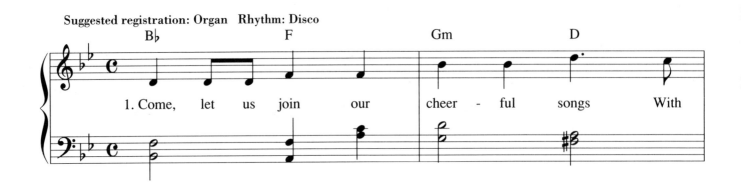

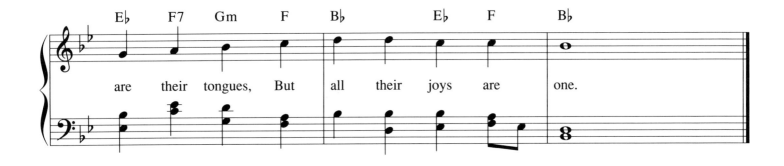

2. "Worthy the Lamb that died," they cry,
   "To be exalted thus!"
   "Worthy the Lamb!" our lips reply,
   "For he was slain for us."

3. Jesus is worthy to receive
   Honour and power divine;
   And blessings, more than we can give,
   Be, Lord, for ever thine.

4. Let all creation join in one
   To bless the sacred name
   Of him that sits upon the throne,
   And to adore the Lamb.

Go Down, Moses

Music: Spiritual, Traditional

Suggested registration: Choir   Rhythm: 8 beat

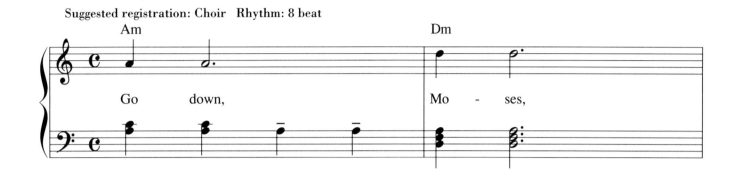

Go down, Mo - ses,

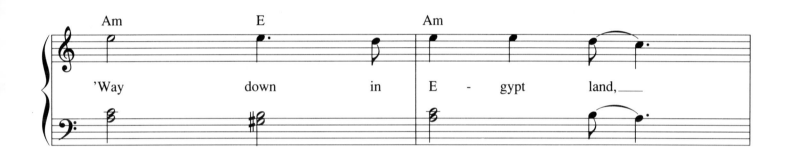

'Way down in E - gypt land,___

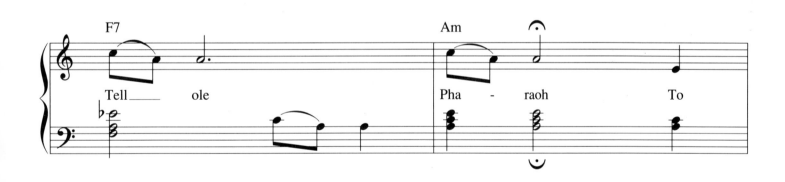

Tell___ ole Pha - raoh To

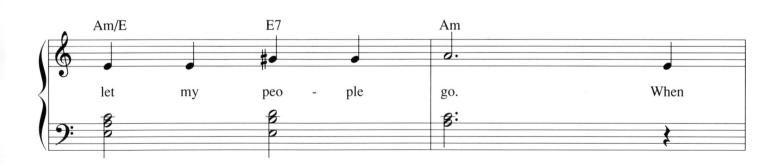

let my peo - ple go. When

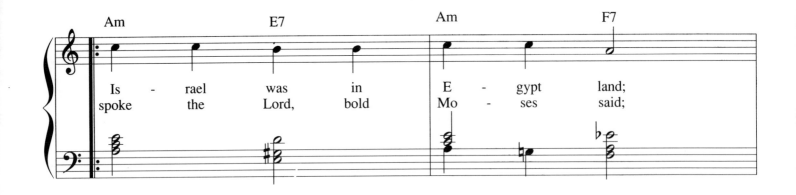

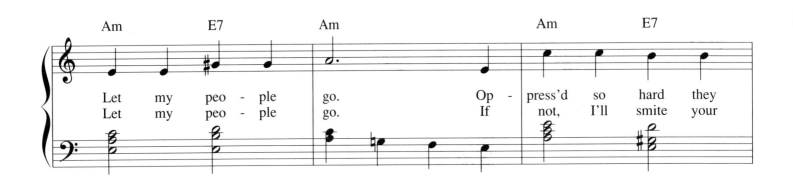

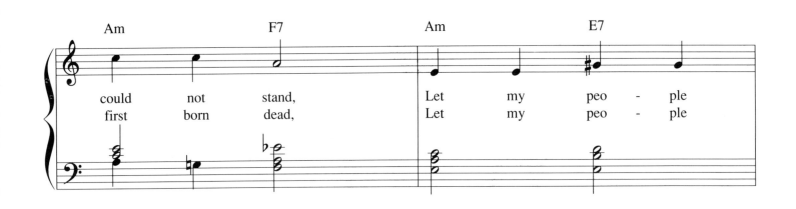

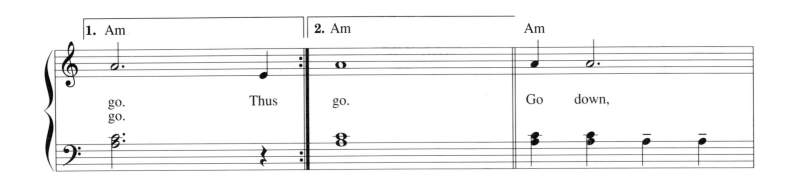

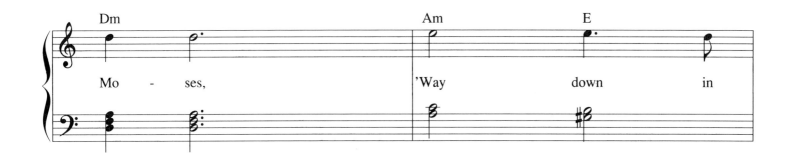

Mo - ses, 'Way down in

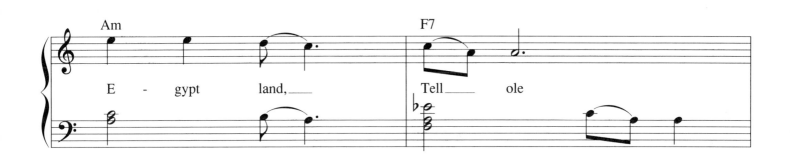

E - gypt land,_____ Tell_____ ole

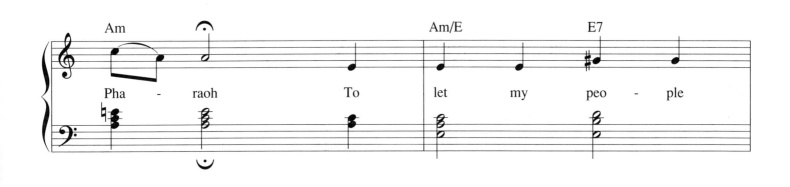

Pha - raoh To let my peo - ple

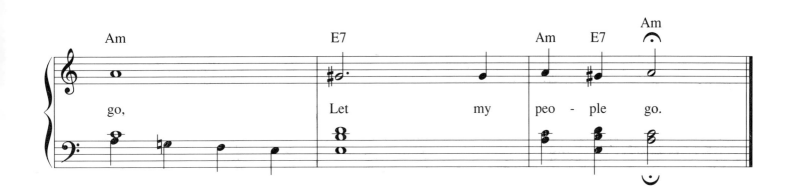

go, Let my peo - ple go.

Give To Our God

Music: F. Duckworth (1862-1941)
Words: Isaac Watts (1674-1748)

Suggested registration: Organ   Rhythm: Waltz

1. Give to our God im - mor - tal

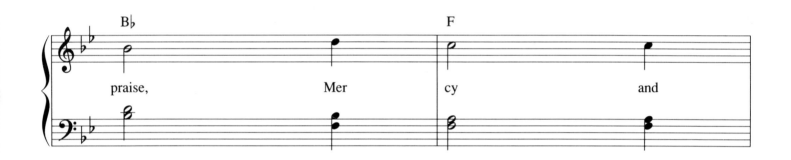

praise, Mer cy and

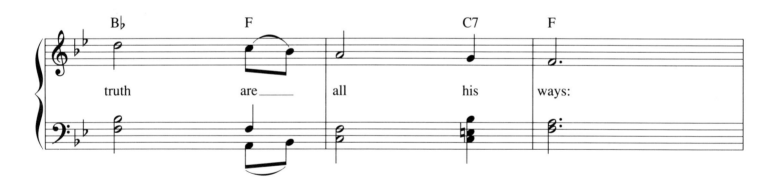

truth are all his ways:

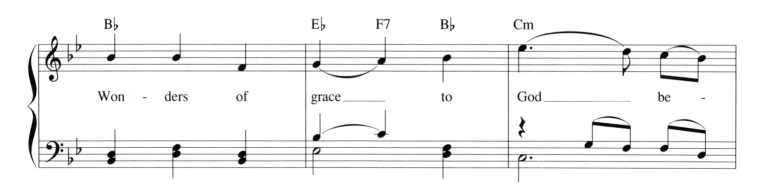

Won - ders of grace to God be -

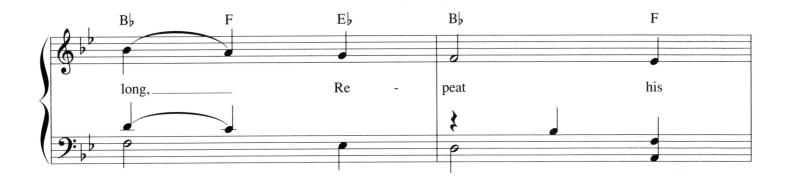

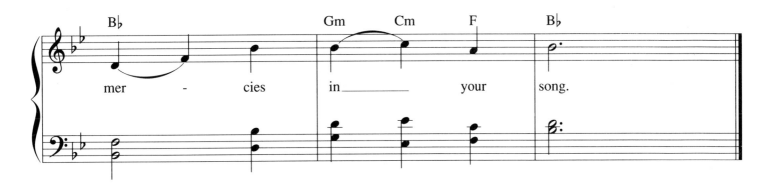

2. Give to the Lord of lords renown,
   The King of kings with glory crown:
   His mercies ever shall endure,
   When lords and kings are known no more.

3. He built the earth, he spread the sky,
   And fixed the starry lights on high:
   Wonders of grace to God belong,
   Repeat his mercies in your song.

4. He fills the sun with morning light,
   He bids the moon direct the night:
   His mercies ever shall endure,
   When suns and moons shall shine no more.

5. He sent his son with power to save
   From guilt and darkness and the grave:
   Wonders of grace to God belong,
   Repeat his mercies in your song.

6. Through this vain world he guides our feet,
   And leads us to his heavenly seat:
   His mercies ever shall endure,
   When this vain world shall be no more.

Hail, To The Lord's Anointed

Music: Adapted by W. H. Monk (1823-89) from a chorale by J Crüger (1598-1662)
Words: James Montgomery (1771-1854)

Suggested registration: Piano   Rhythm: Disco

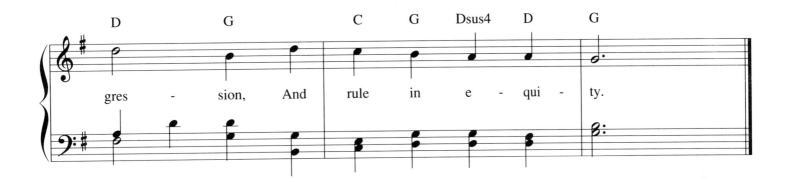

D   G   C   G   Dsus4   D   G

gres - sion, And rule in e - qui - ty.

2. He comes, with succour speedy,
   To those who suffer wrong;
   To help the poor and needy,
   And bid the weak be strong;
   To give them songs for sighing,
   Their darkness turn to light,
   Whose souls, condemned and dying,
   Were precious in his sight.

3. He shall come down like showers
   Upon the fruitful earth;
   Love, joy, and hope, like flowers,
   Spring in his path to birth;
   Before him, on the mountains,
   Shall peace the herald go;
   And righteousness, in fountains,
   From hill to valley flow.

4. Kings shall fall down before Him,
   And gold and incense bring;
   All nations shall adore Him,
   His praise all people sing;
   To him shall prayer unceasing
   And daily vows ascend,
   His kingdom still increasing,
   A kingdom without end.

5. O'er every foe victorious,
   He on his throne shall rest;
   From age to age more glorious,
   All-blessing and all-blessed.
   The tide of time shall never
   His covenant remove;
   His name shall stand for ever,
   His changeless name of love.

Holy, Holy, Holy

Music: J. B. Dykes (1823-1876)
Words: Reginald Heber (1783-1826)

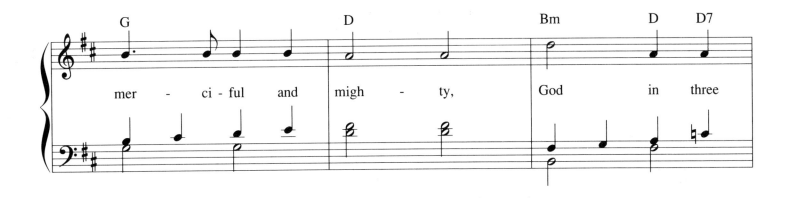

mer - ci - ful and migh - ty, God in three

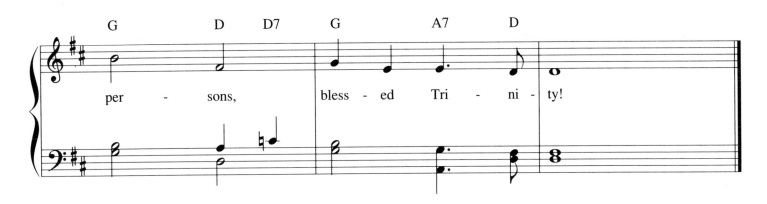

per - sons, bless - ed Tri - ni - ty!

2. Holy, holy, holy! All the saints adore Thee,
   Casting down their golden crowns around the glassy sea;
   Cherubim and Seraphim falling down before Thee,
   Who wert, and art, and evermore shall be.

3. Holy, holy, holy! Though the darkness hides Thee,
   Though the eye of sinful man Thy glory may not see,
   Only Thou art holy; there is none beside Thee,
   Perfect in power, in love, and purity.

4. Holy, holy, holy, Lord God Almighty!
   All Thy works shall praise Thy name in earth and sky and sea;
   Holy, holy, holy, merciful and mighty,
   God in three persons, blessed Trinity!

I Heard The Voice Of Jesus Say

Music: J.B. Dykes (1823-1876)
Words: Horatius Bonar (1808-1889)

Suggested registration: Piano   Rhythm: No rhythm

1. I heard the voice of

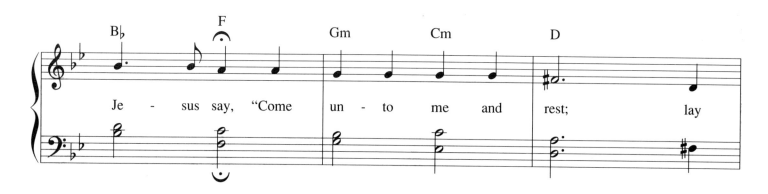

Je - sus say, "Come un - to me and rest; lay

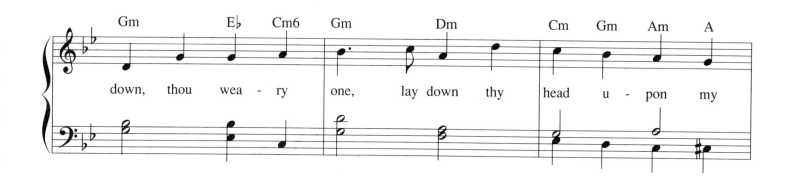

down, thou wea - ry one, lay down thy head u - pon my

8 beat

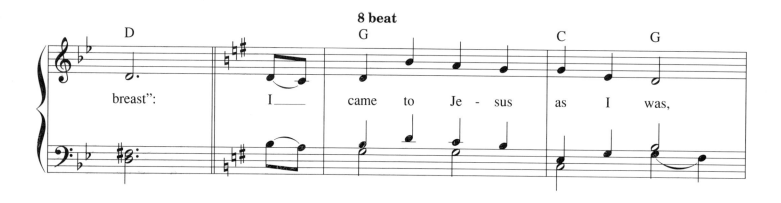

breast": I___ came to Je - sus as I was,

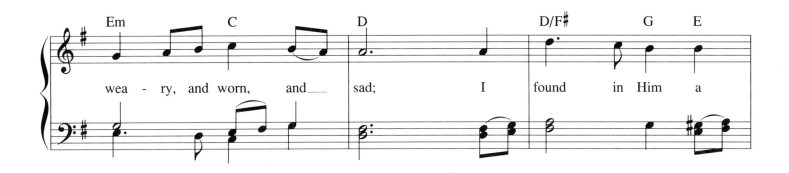

wea - ry, and worn, and___ sad; I found in Him a

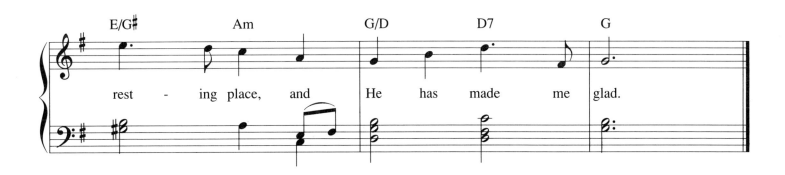

rest - ing place, and He has made me glad.

2. I heard the voice of Jesus say,
   "Behold, I freely give
   The living water; thirsty one,
   Stoop down and drink and live";
   I came to Jesus, and I drank
   Of that life-giving stream;
   My thirst was quenched, my soul revived,
   And now I live in him.

3. I heard the voice of Jesus say,
   "I am this dark world's light;
   Look unto me, thy morn shall rise,
   And all that day be bright":
   I looked to Jesus and I found
   In Him my star, my sun;
   And in that light of life I'll walk
   Till travelling days are done.

It Passeth Knowledge

Music: I.D. Sankey (1840-1908)
Words: Mary Shekleton (1827-1883)

Suggested registration: Piano   Rhythm: 8 beat

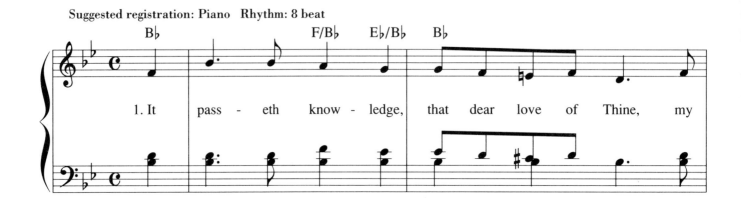

1. It pass - eth know - ledge, that dear love of Thine, my

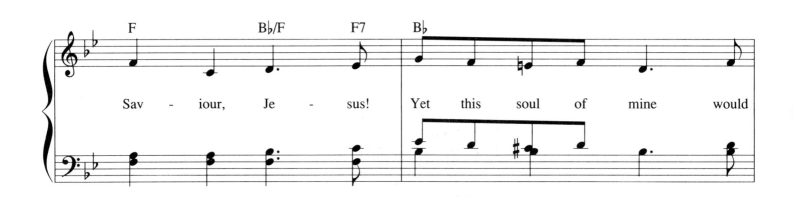

Sav - iour, Je - sus! Yet this soul of mine would

of Thy love, in all its breadth and length, its height and depth, and

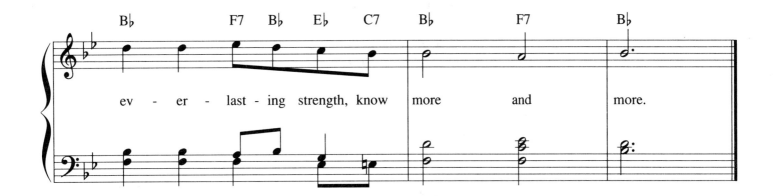

ev - er - last - ing strength, know more and more.

2. It passeth telling, that dear love of Thine,
   My Saviour, Jesus! Yet these lips of mine
   Would fain proclaim, to sinners, far and near,
   A love which can remove all guilty fear,
   And love beget.

3. It passeth praises, that dear love of Thine,
   My Saviour, Jesus! Yet this heart of mine
   Would sing that love, so full, so rich, so free,
   Which brings a rebel sinner, such as me,
   Nigh unto God.

4. O fill me, Saviour, Jesus, with Thy love;
   Lead, lead me to the living fount above;
   Thither may I, in simple faith, draw nigh,
   And never to another fountain fly,
   But unto Thee.

5. And then, when Jesus face to face I see,
   When at His lofty throne I bow the knee,
   Then of His love, in all its breadth and length,
   Its height and depth, its everlasting strength,
   My soul shall sing.

Jerusalem

Music: C.H. Parry (1848-1918
Words: William Blake (1759-1827)

Suggested registration: Organ   Rhythm: Waltz

on our cloud - ed hills? And was Je - ru - sa - lem build - ed

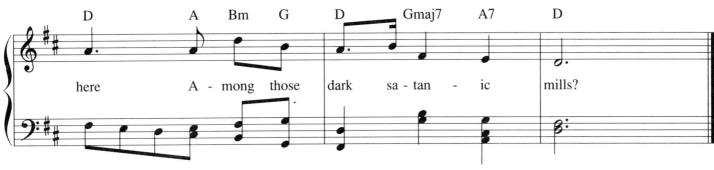

here A - mong those dark sa - tan - ic mills?

2. Bring me my bow of burning gold!
Bring me my arrows of desire!
Bring me my spear! O clouds, unfold!
Bring me my chariot of fire!
I will not cease from mental fight,
Nor shall my sword sleep in my hand,
Till we have built Jerusalem
In England's green and pleasant land.

Jesus Lives

Music: Henry John Gauntlett (1805-1876)
Words: Christian F. Gellert (1715-1769)
Tr: Frances Elizabeth Cox (1812-1897)

Suggested registration: Organ   Rhythm: 8 beat

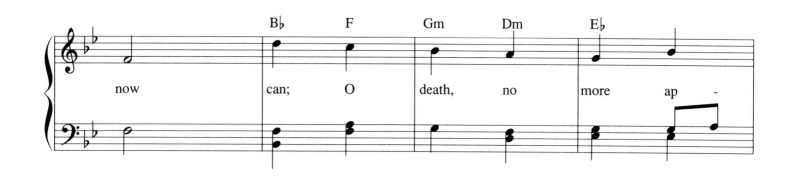

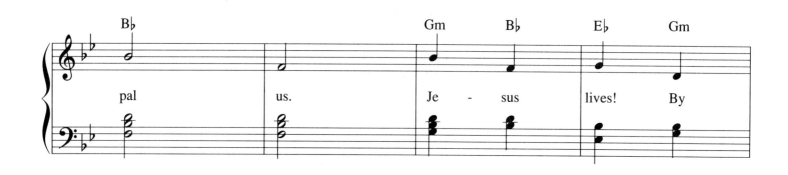

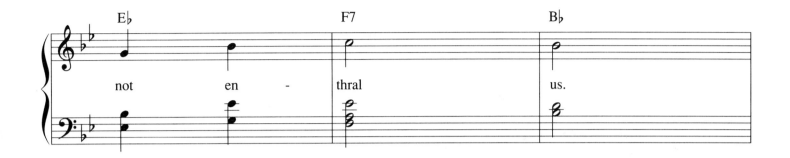

not en - thral us.

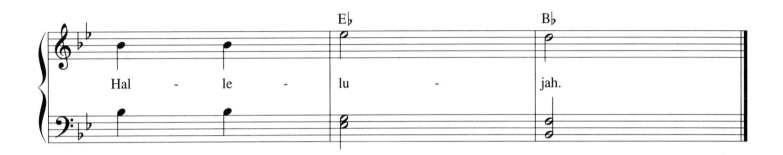

Hal - le - lu - jah.

2. Jesus lives! Henceforth is death
But the gate of life immortal;
This shall calm our trembling breath,
When we pass its gloomy portal.
Hallelujah!

3. Jesus lives! For us he died;
Then, alone to Jesus living,
Pure in heart we may abide,
Glory to our Saviour giving,
Hallelujah!

4. Jesus lives! Our hearts know well,
Naught from us His love shall sever;
Life, nor death, nor powers of hell,
Tear us from His keeping ever.
Hallelujah!

5. Jesus lives! To Him the throne
Over all the world is given:
May we go where He is gone,
Rest and reign with Him in heaven.
Hallelujah!

Jesus Loves Me!

Music: W.B. Bradbury (1816-1868)
Words: Anna Warner (1824-1910)

Suggested registration: Piano   Rhythm: 8 beat

1. Je - sus loves me! This I know,

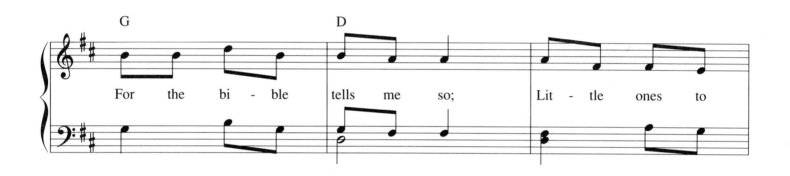

For the bi - ble tells me so; Lit - tle ones to

Him be - long; They are weak but,

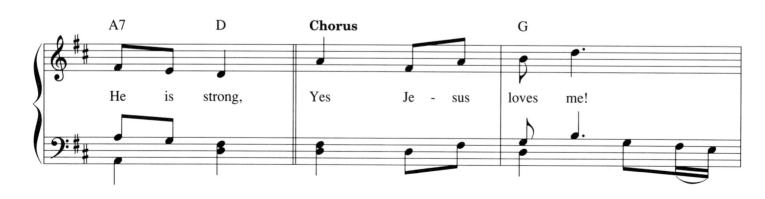

He is strong, Yes Je - sus loves me!

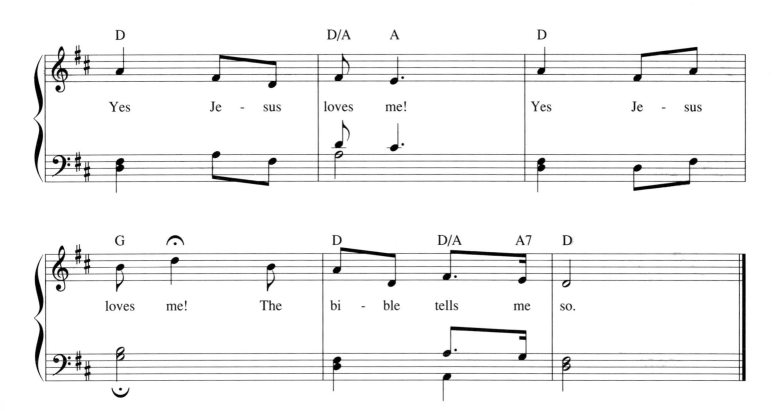

Yes   Je - sus   loves   me!   Yes   Je - sus
loves   me!   The   bi - ble   tells   me   so.

2. Jesus loves me! He who died
   Heaven's gate to open wide;
   He will wash away my sin:
   Let his little child come in.

   Chorus

3. Jesus loves me! He will stay
   Close beside me all the way;
   If I love Him, when I die
   He will take me home on high.

   Chorus

4. Jesus, take this heart of mine,
   Make it pure and wholly thine;
   Thou hast bled and died for me,
   I will henceforth live for Thee.

   Chorus

Jesus Shall Reign

Music: From '*Psalmodia Evangelica*', 1789
Words: Isaac Watts (1674-1748)

2. For Him shall endless prayer be made,
And praises throng to crown His head;
His name like sweet perfume shall rise
With every morning sacrifice.

3. People and realms of every tongue
Dwell on His love with sweetest song;
And infant voices shall proclaim
Their early blessings on his name.

4. Blessings abound where'er He reigns;
The prisoner leaps to lose His chains;
The weary find eternal rest,
And all the sons of want are blessed.

5. Let every creature rise and bring
Peculiar honours to our King;
Angels descend with songs again,
And earth repeat the loud amen.

In The Cross Of Christ

Music: J. B. Dykes (1823-76)
Words: John Bowring (1792-1872)

2. When the woes of life o'ertake me,
   Hopes deceive and fears annoy,
   Never shall the cross forsake me,
   Lo, it glows with peace and joy.

3. When the sun of bliss is beaming
   Light and love upon my way,
   From the cross the radiance streaming
   Adds more lustre to the day.

4. Bane and blessing, pain and pleasure,
   By the cross are sanctified;
   Peace is there that knows no measure,
   Joys that through all time abide.

5. In the cross of Christ I glory:
   Tow'ring o'er the wrecks of time,
   All the light of sacred story
   Gathers round its head sublime.

Joshua Fought The Battle Of Jericho

Music: Spiritual, Traditional

Suggested registration: Electric guitar   Rhythm: Rock

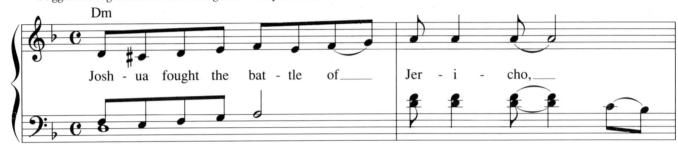

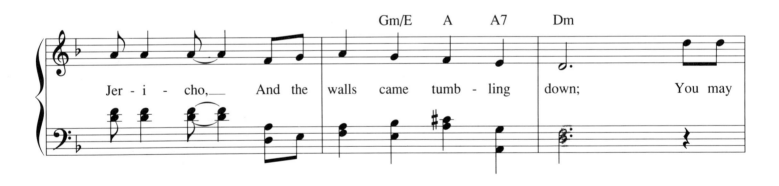

Judge Eternal

Music: Welsh traditional melody
Words: Henry Scott Holland (1847-1918) altered

2. Still the weary folk are pining
   For the hour that brings release;
   And the city's crowded clangour
   Cries aloud for sin to cease;
   And the homesteads and the woodlands
   Plead in silence for their peace.

3. Crown, O God, your own endeavour;
   Cleave our darkness with your sword;
   Feed the faithless and the hungry
   With the richness of your word;
   Cleanse the body of this nation
   Through the glory of the Lord.

Just As I Am, Without One Plea

Music: Henry Smart (1813-79)
Words: Charlotte Elliott (1789-1871)

Suggested registration: Piano   Rhythm: Waltz

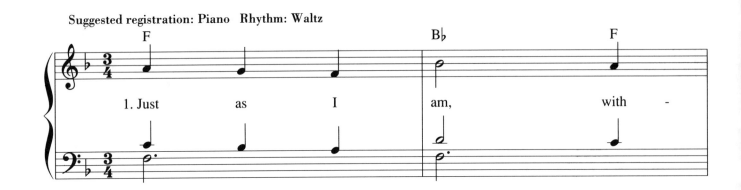

1. Just as I am, with -

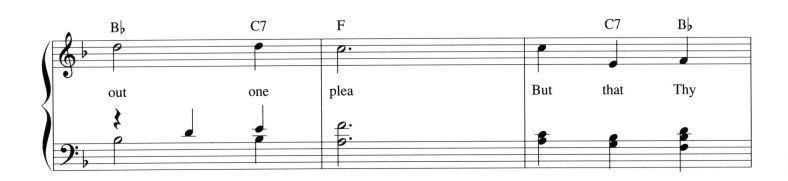

out one plea But that Thy

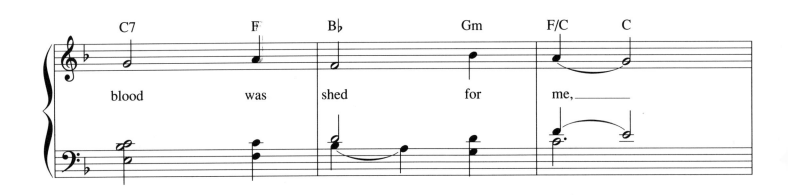

blood was shed for me,____

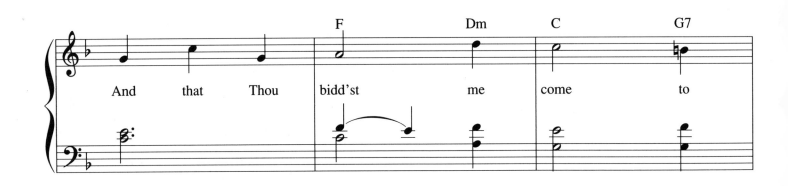

And that Thou bidd'st me come to

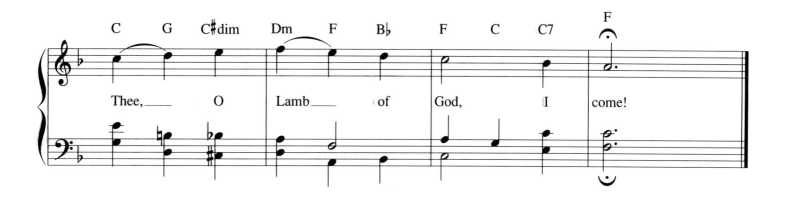

Thee,____ O Lamb____ of God, I come!

2. Just as I am, though tossed about
   With many a conflict, many a doubt,
   Fightings and fears within, without,
   O Lamb of God, I come!

3. Just as I am, poor, wretched, blind;
   Sight, riches, healing of the mind,
   Because Thy promise I believe,
   O Lamb of God, I come!

4. Just as I am, Thou wilt receive,
   Wilt welcome, pardon, cleanse, relieve;
   Because Thy promise I believe
   O Lamb of God, I come!

5. Just as I am, Thy love unknown
   Has broken every barrier down,
   Now to be Thine, yea, Thine alone,
   O Lamb of God, I come!

6. Just as I am, of that free love
   The breadth, length, depth, and height to prove,
   Here for a season, then above,
   O Lamb of God, I come!

Lead Us, Heavenly Father, Lead Us

Music: F. Filitz (1804-1876)
Words: James Edmeston (1791-1867)

Suggested registration: Organ   Rhythm: 8 beat

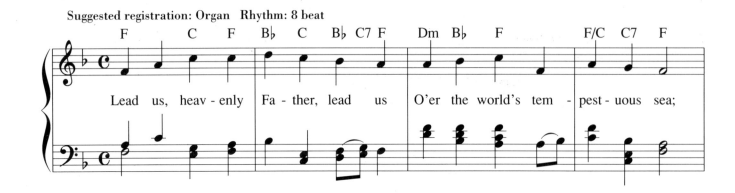

Lead us, heav - enly Fa - ther, lead us O'er the world's tem - pest - uous sea;

Guard us, guide us, keep us, feed us, For we have no help but thee.

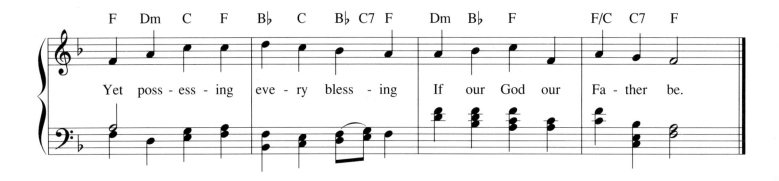

Yet poss - ess - ing eve - ry bless - ing If our God our Fa - ther be.

2. Saviour, breathe forgiveness o'er us;
   All our weakness Thou dost know,
   Thou didst tread this earth before us,
   Thou didst feel its keenest woe;
   Tempted, taunted, yet undaunted,
   Through the desert Thou didst go.

3. Spirit of our God, descending,
   Fill our hearts with heavenly joy,
   Love with every passion blending,
   Pleasure that can never cloy;
   Thus provided, pardoned, guided,
   Nothing can our peace destroy.

Let Us With A Gladsome Mind

Music: John Antes (1740-1811)
arr. John Wilkes (1785-1869)
Words: John Milton (1608-1674)

Suggested registration: Organ Rhythm: 8 beat

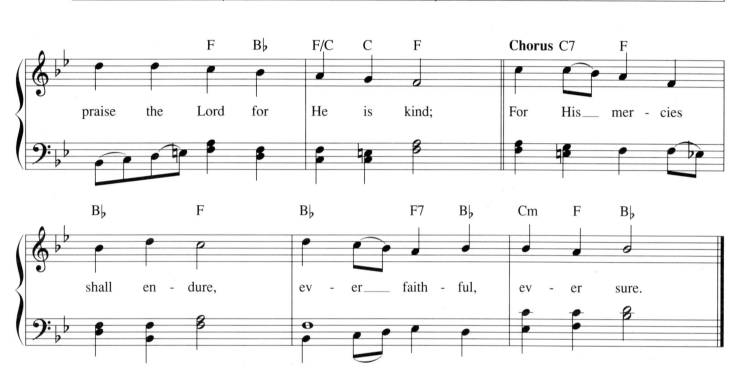

2. He, with all commanding might,
   Filled the new-made world with light:

   Chorus

3. All things living He doth feed,
   His full hand supplies their need:

   Chorus

4. He, His chosen race did bless
   In the wasteland wilderness:

   Chorus

5. He hath, with a piteous eye,
   Looked upon our misery:

   Chorus

6. Let us then with gladsome mind,
   Praise the Lord for He is kind!

Like A River Glorious

Music: J. Mountain (1844-1933)
Words: Frances Ridley Havergal (1836-1879)

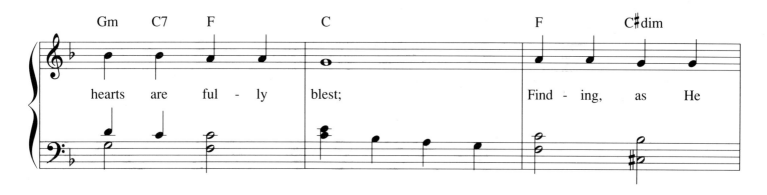

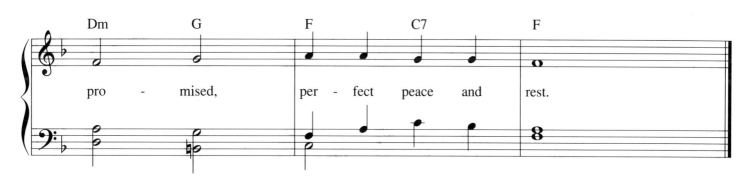

2. Hidden in the hollow
   Of his blessed hand,
   Never foe can follow
   Never traitor stand;
   Not a surge of worry,
   Not a shade of care,
   Not a blast of hurry
   Touch the Spirit there.

   Chorus

3. Every joy or trial
   Falleth from above,
   Traced upon our dial
   By the sun of love.
   We may trust Him fully
   All for us to do;
   They who trust Him wholly
   Find Him wholly true.

   Chorus

Look, Ye Saints

Music: H. J. Gauntlett (1805-1876)
Words: Thomas Kelly (1769-1854)

Suggested registration: Organ   Rhythm: Rock

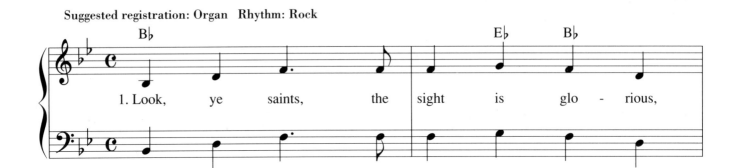

1. Look, ye saints, the sight is glo - rious,

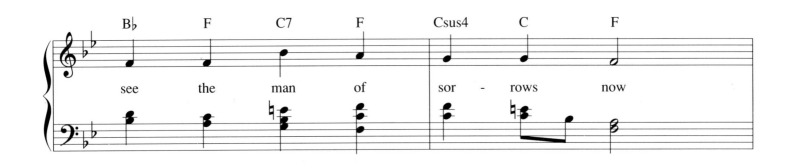

see the man of sor - rows now

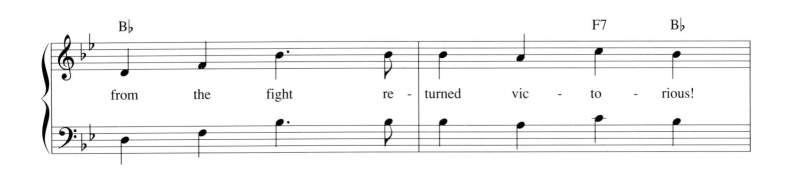

from the fight re - turned vic - to - rious!

Ev - 'ry knee to Him shall bow:

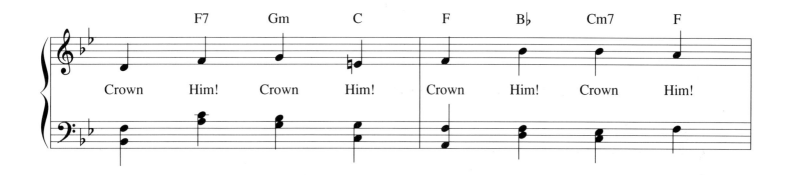

F7   Gm   C   F   B♭   Cm7   F

Crown   Him!   Crown   Him!   Crown   Him!   Crown   Him!

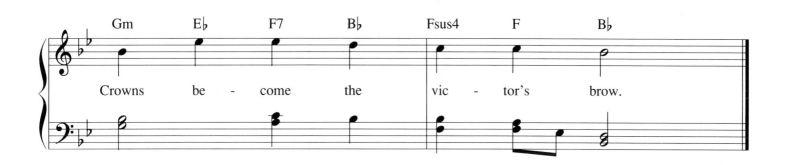

Gm   E♭   F7   B♭   Fsus4   F   B♭

Crowns   be - come   the   vic - tor's   brow.

2. Crown the Saviour, angels, crown Him!
   Rich the trophies Jesus brings;
   In the seat of power enthrone Him,
   While the vault of heaven rings:
   Crown Him! Crown Him!
   Crown Him! Crown Him!
   Crown the Saviour King of kings!

3. Sinners in derision crowned Him,
   Mocking thus the Saviour's claim;
   Saints and angels crowd around Him,
   Own His title, praise His name:
   Crown Him! Crown Him!
   Crown Him! Crown Him!
   Spread abroad the victor's fame.

4. Hark, those bursts of acclamation!
   Hark, those loud triumphant chords!
   Jesus takes the highest station:
   O what joy the sight affords!
   Crown Him! Crown Him!
   Crown Him! Crown Him!
   King of kings and Lord of lords!

Love Divine

Music: W. P. Rowlands (1860-1937)
Words: Charles Wesley (1707-1788)

Suggested registration: Electric piano   Rhythm: Waltz

2. Come, almighty to deliver,
   Let us all Thy life receive;
   Suddenly return and never,
   Never more Thy temples leave.
   Thee we would be always blessing,
   Serve Thee as Thy hosts above,
   Pray, and praise Thee, without ceasing,
   Glory in your perfect love.

3. Finish then Thy new creation,
   Pure and spotless let us be;
   Let us see Thy great salvation,
   Perfectly restored in Thee:
   Changed from glory into glory,
   Till in heaven we take our place,
   Till we cast our crowns before Thee,
   Lost in wonder, love, and praise!

Loved With Everlasting Love

Music: James Mountain (1843-1933)
Words: George Wade Robinson (1838-1877)

Suggested registration: Organ Rhythm: No rhythm

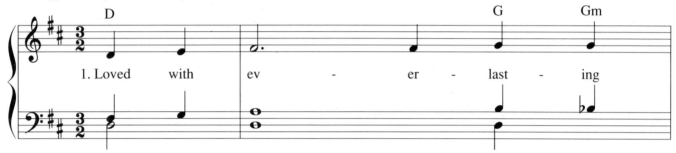

1. Loved with ev - er - last - ing

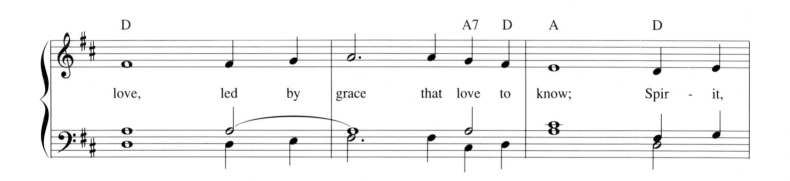

love, led by grace that love to know; Spir - it,

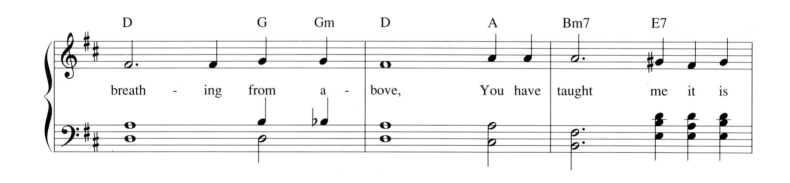

breath - ing from a - bove, You have taught me it is

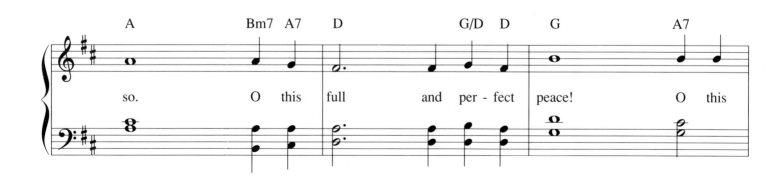

so. O this full and per - fect peace! O this

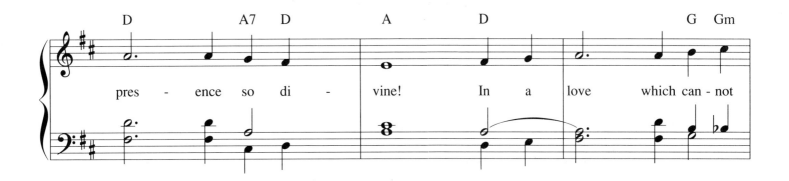

pres - ence so di - vine! In a love which can - not

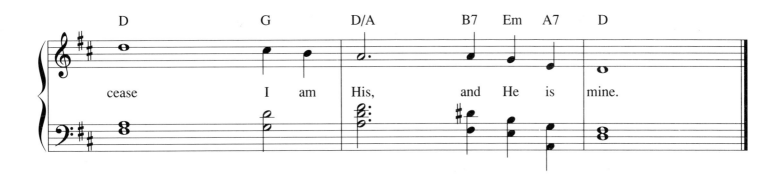

cease I am His, and He is mine.

2. Heaven above is softer blue,
   Earth around is sweeter green;
   Something lives in every hue,
   Christless eyes have never seen:
   Birds with gladder songs o'erflow,
   Flowers with deeper beauties shine,
   Since I know, as I now know,
   I am His, and He is mine.

3. His for ever, only His:
   Who the Lord and me shall part?
   Ah, with what a rest of bliss
   Christ can fill the loving heart!
   Heaven and earth may fade and flee,
   First-born light in gloom decline;
   But while God and I shall be,
   I am His, and He is mine.

Low In The Grave He Lay

Words and Music: Robert Lowry (1826-1899)

Suggested registration: Organ   Rhythm: No rhythm

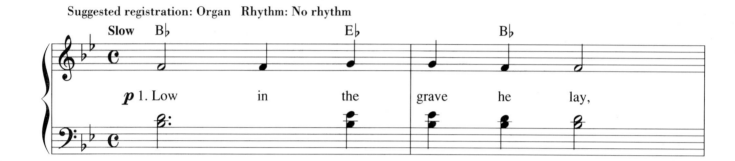

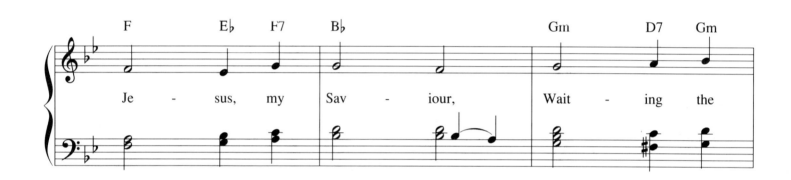

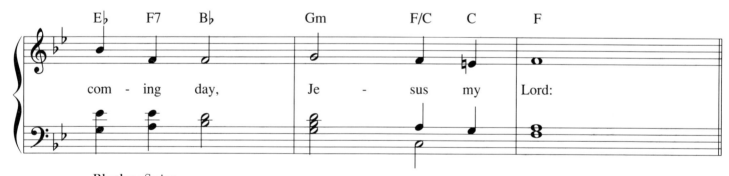

Rhythm: Swing
Suggested registration: Piano
Faster
Refrain

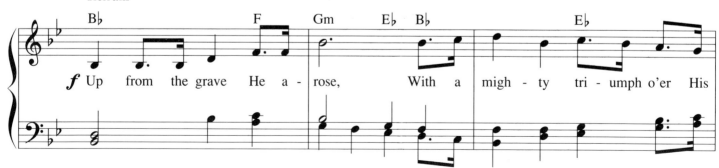

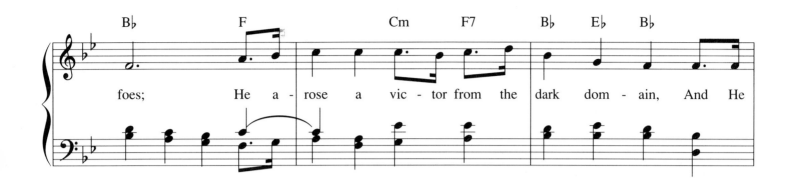

foes; He a - rose a vic - tor from the dark dom - ain, And He

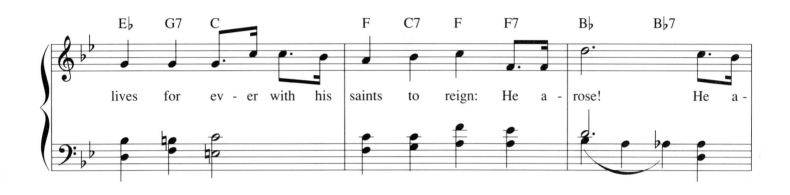

lives for ev - er with his saints to reign: He a - rose! He a -

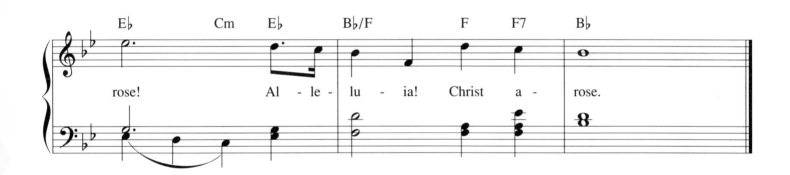

rose! Al - le - lu - ia! Christ a - rose.

2. Vainly they watch his bed,
   Jesus, my Saviour;
   Vainly they seal the dead,
   Jesus, my Lord:

Refrain

3. Death cannot keep his prey,
   Jesus, my saviour;
   He tore the bars away,
   Jesus, my Lord:

Refrain

Nobody Knows The Trouble I've Seen

Music: Spiritual, Traditional

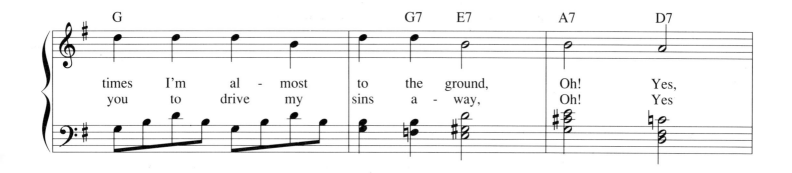

times I'm al - most   to the ground,   Oh!   Yes,
you to drive my   sins a - way,   Oh!   Yes

Lord. _____

Lord. _____   Oh,   no - bo - dy knows   the   trou - ble I've   seen,

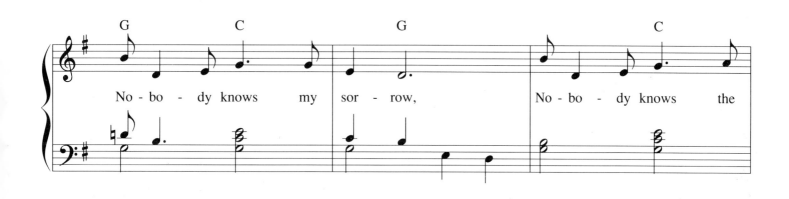

No - bo - dy knows   my   sor - row,   No - bo - dy knows   the

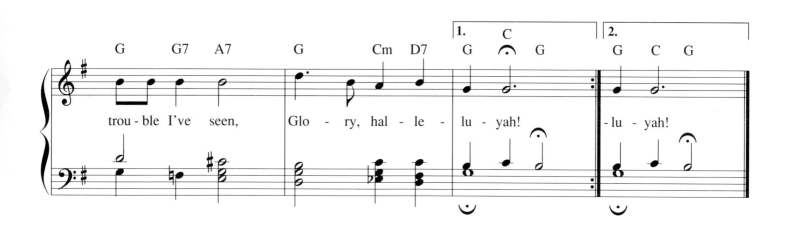

trou - ble I've   seen,   Glo - ry, hal - le - lu - yah!   -lu - yah!

Now Thank We All Our God

Music: J. Crüger (1598-1662)
Words: Martin Rinkart (1586-1649), Tr. Catherine Winkworth (1829-1878)

Suggested registration: Organ   Rhythm: 8 beat

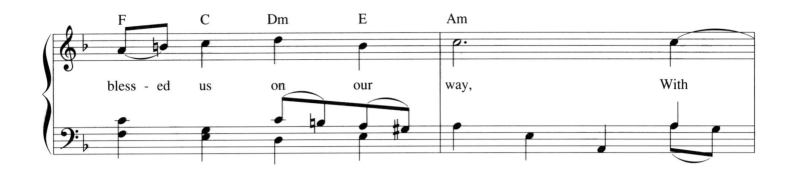

bless - ed us on our way, With

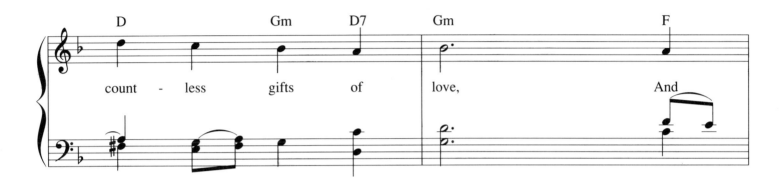

count - less gifts of love, And

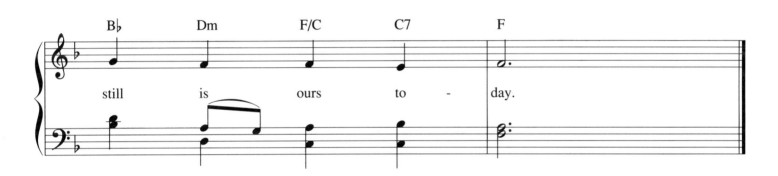

still is ours to - day.

2. O may this bounteous God
   Through all our life be near us,
   With ever joyful hearts
   And blessed peace to cheer us;
   And keep us in his grace,
   And guide us when perplexed,
   And free us from all ills
   In this world and the next.

3. All praise and thanks to God
   The Father now be given,
   The Son, and Him who reigns
   With them in highest heaven,
   The one eternal God,
   Whom heaven and earth adore,
   For thus it was, is now,
   And shall be evermore.

O For A Thousand Tongues

Music: T. Jarman (1782-1862)
Words: Charles Wesley (1707-1788) (altered)

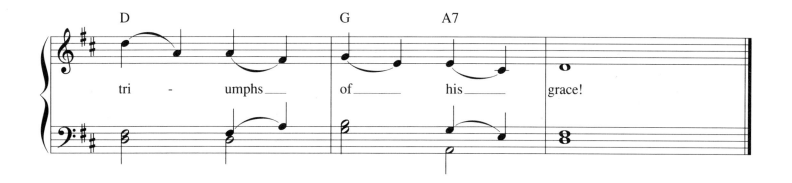

tri - umphs___ of___ his___ grace!

2. My gracious Master and my God,
   Assist me to proclaim,
   To spread through all the earth abroad
   The honours of Thy name.

3. Jesus - the name that charms our fears,
   That bids our sorrows cease;
   'Tis music in the sinner's ears,
   'Tis life, and health, and peace.

4. He breaks the power of cancelled sin,
   He sets the prisoner free;
   His blood can make the foulest clean,
   His blood availed for me.

5. He speaks; and, listening to His voice,
   New life the dead receive;
   The mournful, broken hearts rejoice;
   The humble poor believe.

6. Hear him, ye deaf; His praise, ye dumb,
   Your loosened tongues employ;
   Ye blind, behold your saviour come;
   And leap, ye lame, for joy!

7. See all your sins on Jesus laid:
   The Lamb of God was slain;
   His soul was once an offering made
   For every soul of man.

8. In Christ, our Head, you then shall know,
   Shall feel, your sins forgiven,
   Anticipate your heaven below,
   And own that love is heaven.

O Love That Wilt Not Let Me Go

Music: A. L. Peace (1844-1912)
Words: George Matheson (1842-1906)

Suggested registration: Piano   Rhythm: No rhythm

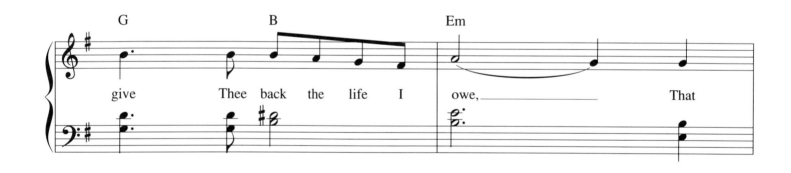

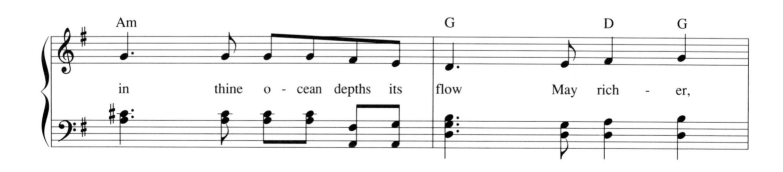

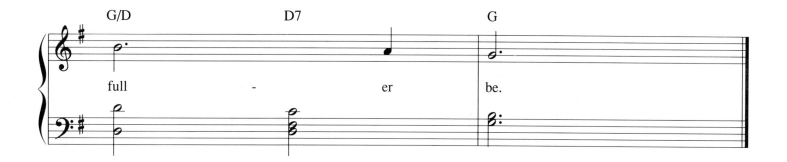

2. O light that followest all my way,
   I yield my flickering torch to Thee:
   My heart restores its borrowed ray,
   That in Thy sunshine's blaze its day
   May brighter, fairer be.

3. O joy that seekest me through pain,
   I cannot close my heart to Thee:
   I trace the rainbow through the rain,
   And feel the promise is not vain,
   That morn shall tearless be.

4. O cross that liftest up my head,
   I dare not ask to fly from Thee:
   I lay in dust life's glory dead,
   And from the ground there blossoms red
   Life that shall endless be.

O Worship The King

Music: A Supplement To The New Version 1708, probably by W. Croft (1678-1727)
Words: From Psalm 104 after W. Kethe (died 1594), R. Grant (1779-1838)

Suggested registration: Flute   Rhythm: Waltz

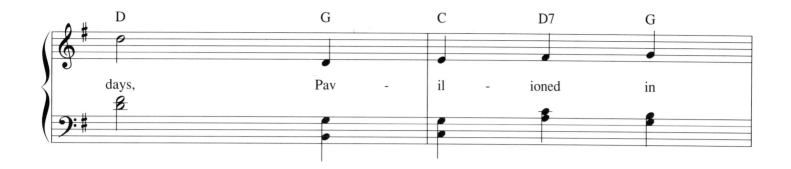

days,   Pav - il - ioned   in

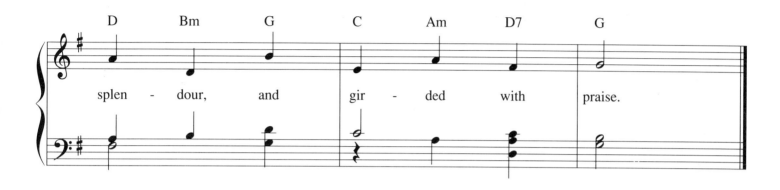

splen - dour,   and   gir - ded   with   praise.

2. O tell of His might, O sing of His grace,
   Whose robe is the light, whose canopy space;
   His chariots of wrath the deep thunder-clouds form,
   And dark is His path on the wings of the storm.

3. The earth with its store of wonders untold,
   Almighty, Thy pow'r hath founded of old;
   Hath 'stablished it fast by a changeless decree,
   And round it hath cast, like a mantle, the sea.

4. Thy bountiful care what tongue can recite?
   It breathes in the air, it shines in the light;
   It swims from the streams, it descends to the plain,
   And sweetly distils in the dew and the rain.

5. Frail children of dust, and feeble as frail,
   In Thee we do trust, nor find Thee to fail;
   Thy mercies how tender, how firm to the end,
   Our maker, defender, Redeemer, and friend.

6. O measureless might, ineffable love,
   While angels delight to hymn Thee above,
   Thy humbler creation, though feeble their lays,
   With true adoration shall sing to Thy praise.

O Worship The Lord

Music: W. H. Cook (1820-1912)
Words: J.S.B. Monsell (1811-1875)

Suggested registration: Electric piano Rhythm: Waltz

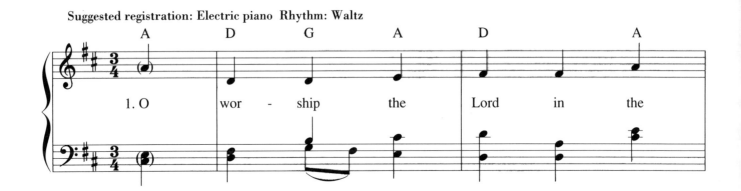

1. O wor - ship the Lord in the

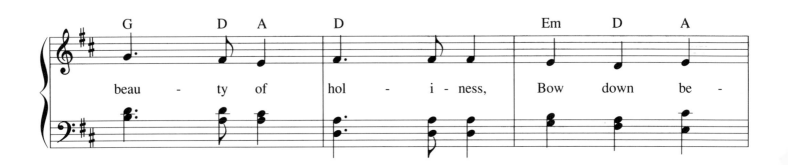

beau - ty of hol - i - ness, Bow down be -

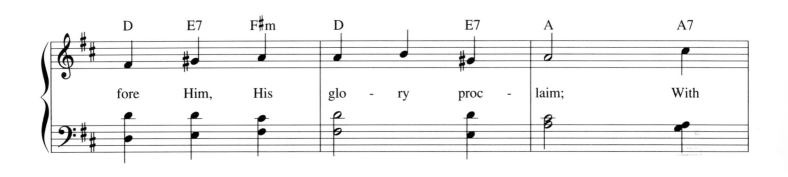

fore Him, His glo - ry proc - laim; With

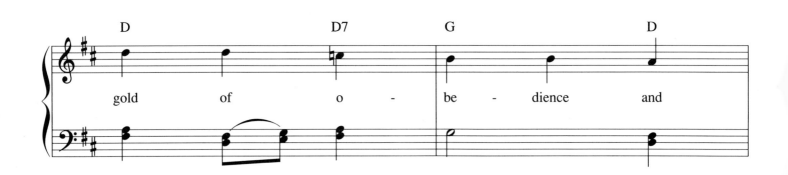

gold of o - be - dience and

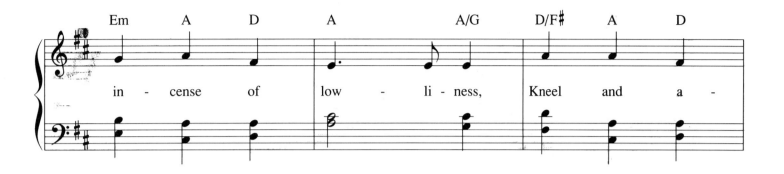

in - cense of low - li - ness, Kneel and a -

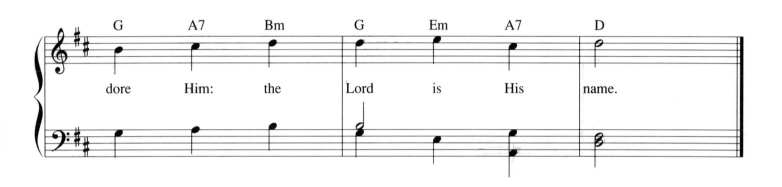

dore Him: the Lord is His name.

2. Low at His feet lay thy burden of carefulness,
   High on His heart He will bear it for thee,
   Comfort thy sorrows, and answer thy prayerfulness,
   Guiding thy steps as may best for thee be.

3. Fear not to enter His courts in the slenderness
   Of the poor wealth thou wouldst reckon as thine;
   Truth in its beauty and love in its tenderness,
   These are the offerings to lay on His shrine.

4. These, though we bring them in trembling and fearfulness,
   He will accept for the name that is dear;
   Mornings of joy give for evenings of tearfulness,
   Trust for our trembling and hope for our fear.

5. O worship the Lord in the beauty of holiness,
   Bow down before Him, His glory proclaim;
   With gold of obedience and incense of lowliness,
   Kneel and adore Him: the Lord is His name.

Onward, Christian Soldiers

Music: Arthur S. Sullivan (1842-1900)
Words: S. Baring-Gould (1834-1924)

Suggested registration: Brass   Rhythm: March

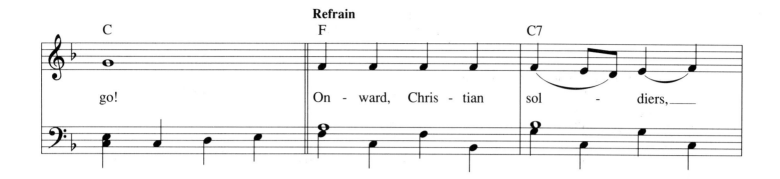

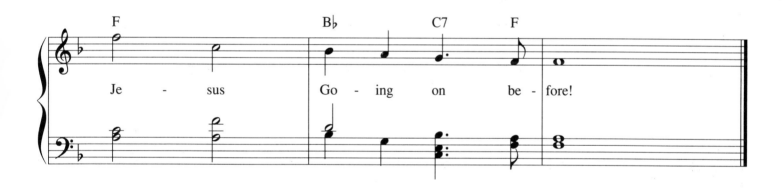

2. At the sign of triumph
   Satan's host doth flee;
   On then, Christian soldiers,
   On to victory!
   Hell's foundations quiver
   At the shout of praise;
   Brothers lift your voices;
   Loud your anthems raise.

   Refrain

3. Crowns and thrones may perish,
   Kingdoms rise and wane,
   But the Church of Jesus
   Constant will remain;
   Gates of hell can never
   'Gainst that Church prevail;
   We have Christ's own promise
   And that cannot fail.

   Refrain

4. Onward, then, ye people!
   Join our happy throng;
   Blend with ours your voices
   In the triumph-song:
   Glory, laud, and honour
   Unto Christ the King!
   This through countless ages
   Men and angels sing:

   Refrain

Praise, My Soul

Music: J. Goss (1800-80)
Words: H. F. Lyte (1793-1847)

Suggested registration: Organ   Rhythm: 8 beat

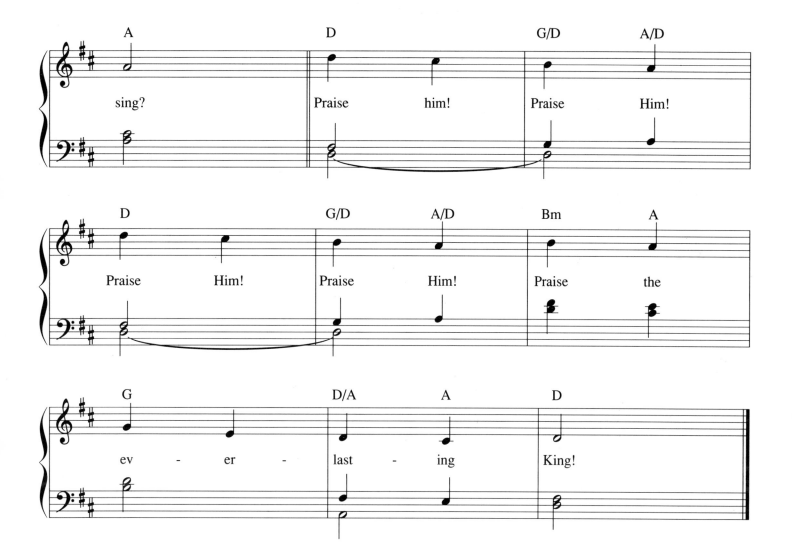

2. Praise Him for His grace and favour
   To our fathers in distress;
   Praise Him, still the same for ever,
   Slow to chide, and swift to bless.
   Praise Him! Praise Him!
   Praise Him! Praise Him!
   Glorious in His faithfulness.

3. Father-like He tends and spares us;
   Well our feeble frame He knows;
   In His hands He gently bears us,
   Rescues us from all our foes.
   Praise Him! Praise Him!
   Praise Him! Praise Him!
   Widely as his mercy flows.

4. Angels in the height, adore Him;
   Ye behold Him face to face;
   Sun and moon, bow down before Him,
   Dwellers all in time and space.
   Praise Him! Praise Him!
   Praise Him! Praise Him!
   Praise with us the God of grace!

Praise The Lord

Music: Franz Joseph Haydn (1732-1809)
Words: Based on Psalm 148

Suggested registration: Brass   Rhythm: 8 beat

1. Praise the Lord! Ye heav'ns adore Him: Praise Him, angels in the height; Praise the Lord, for He hath spoken; Worlds His mighty voice obeyed; Laws that never shall be broken For their guidance He hath made.

Sun and moon, rejoice before Him; Praise Him, all ye stars and light;

2. Praise the Lord, for He hath spoken;
   Never shall His promise fail;
   God hath made His saints victorious;
   Sin and death shall not prevail.

   Praise the God of our salvation;
   Hosts on high, His power proclaim;
   Heaven and earth and all creation,
   Laud and magnify His name!

O Come Let Us Adore Him

Music: J. F. Wade (1711-1786)
Words: J. Wade; F. Oakley and others

Suggested registration: Voices   Rhythm: 8 beat

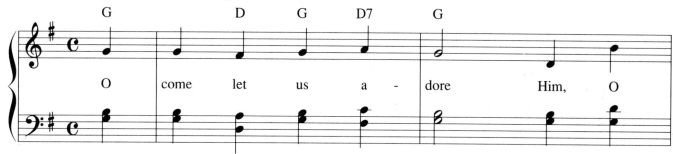

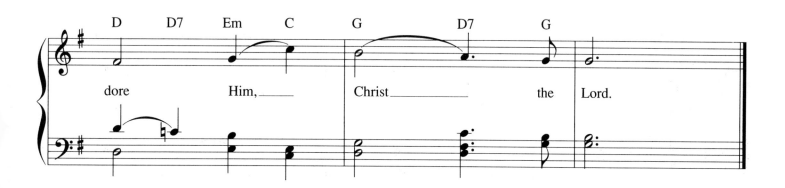

Praise to the Holiest

Music: J. B. Dykes (1823-1876)
Words: J. H. Newman (1801-1890)

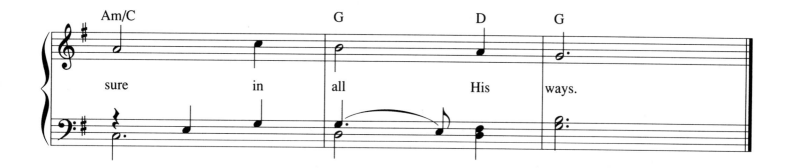

sure   in   all   His   ways.

2. O loving wisdom of our God!
   When all was sin and shame,
   A second Adam to the fight
   And to the rescue came.

3. O wisest love! That flesh and blood,
   Which did in Adam fail,
   Should strive afresh against the foe,
   Should strive and should prevail;

4. And that a higher gift than grace
   Should flesh and blood refine,
   God's presence and His very self,
   And essence all divine.

5. O generous love! That He, who smote
   In man for man the foe,
   The double agony in man
   For man should undergo;

6. And in the garden secretly,
   And on the cross on high,
   Should teach his brethren, and inspire
   To suffer and to die.

7. Praise to the Holiest in the height,
   And in the depth be praise;
   In all His words most wonderful,
   Most sure in all his ways.

Rejoice, The Lord Is King

Music: G. F. Handel (1685-1759)
Words: Charles Wesley (1707-1788)

Suggested registration: Organ   Rhythm: 8 beat

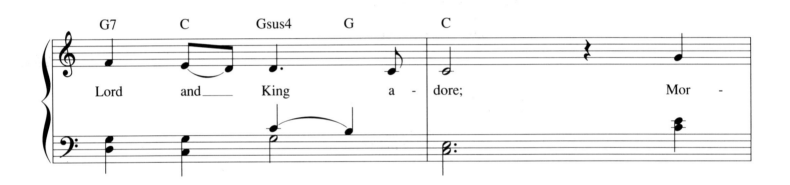

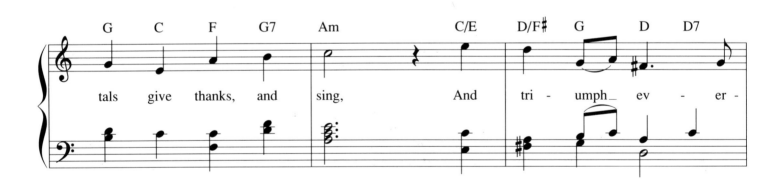

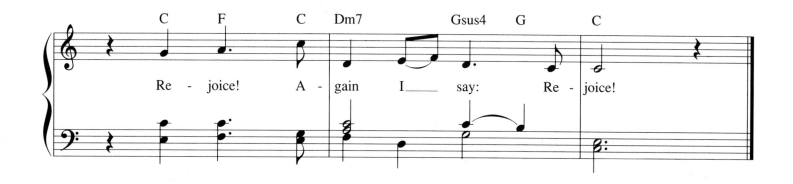

Re - joice! A - gain I___ say: Re - joice!

2. Jesus the Saviour reigns,
   The God of truth and love;
   When He had purged our stains,
   He took his seat above;

   Refrain

3. His kingdom cannot fail,
   He rules o'er earth and heaven;
   The keys of death and hell
   Are to our Jesus given:

   Refrain

4. He sits at God's right hand
   Till all his foes submit,
   And bow to his command,
   And fall beneath his feet;

   Refrain

5. Rejoice in glorious hope;
   Jesus the Judge shall come,
   And take His servants up
   To their eternal home:

   V.5 **Refrain**

We soon shall hear the archangel's voice;
The trump of God shall sound: Rejoice!

Stand Up! Stand Up For Jesus

Music: G. J. Webb (1803-1887)
Words: George Duffield (1818-1888)

Suggested registration: Piano   Rhythm: 8 beat

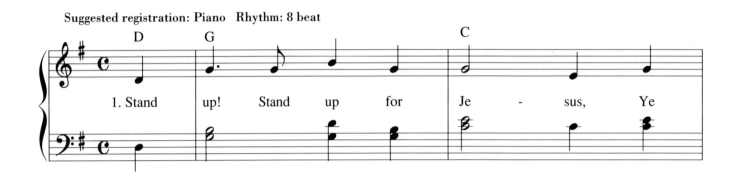

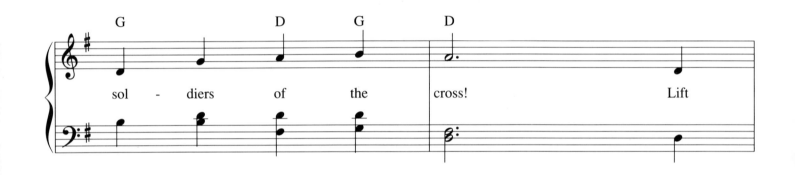

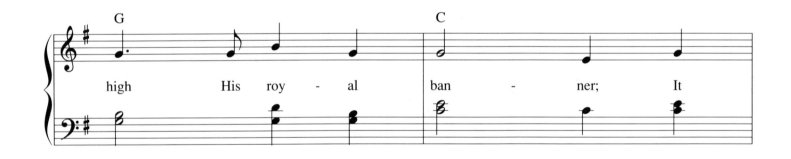

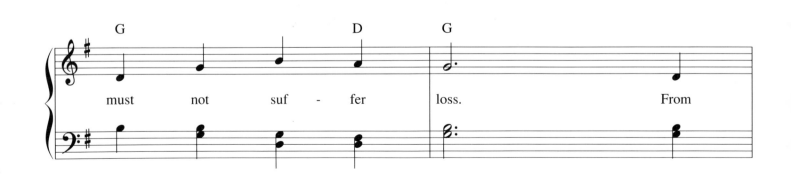

2. Stand up! Stand up for Jesus!
   The trumpet-call obey;
   Forth to the mighty conflict
   In this His glorious day!
   Ye that are His, now serve Him
   Against unnumbered foes;
   Let courage rise with danger,
   And strength to strength oppose.

3. Stand up! Stand up for Jesus!
   Stand in his strength alone;
   The arm of flesh will fail you;
   Ye dare not trust your own.
   Put on the Gospel armour,
   Each piece put on with prayer;
   Where duty calls, or danger,
   Be never wanting there.

4. Stand up! Stand up for Jesus!
   The strife will not be long;
   This day the noise of battle,
   The next the victors' song.
   To Him that overcometh
   A crown of life shall be;
   He with the King of Glory
   Shall reign eternally.

Take My Life

Music: Wolfgang Amadeus Mozart (1756-1791)
Words: Frances Ridley Havergal (1836-1879)

Suggested registration: Strings   Rhythm: Waltz

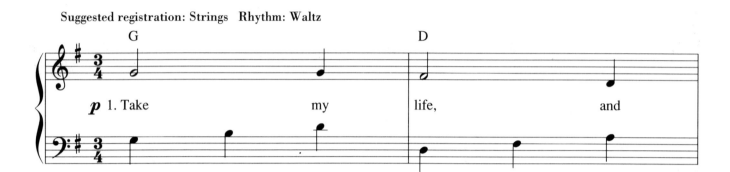

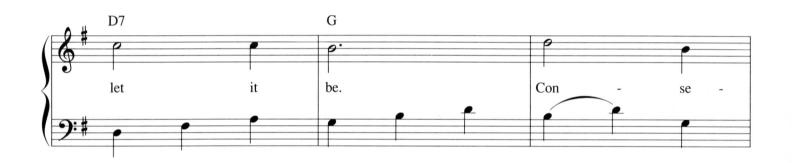

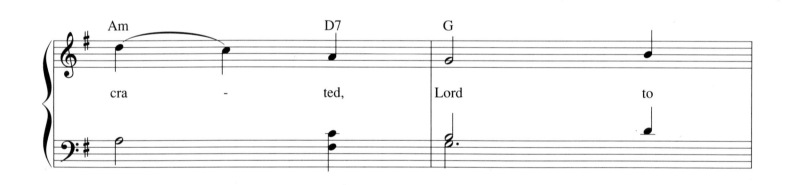

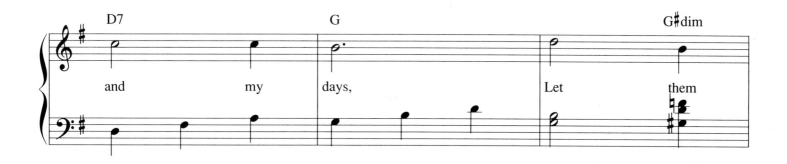

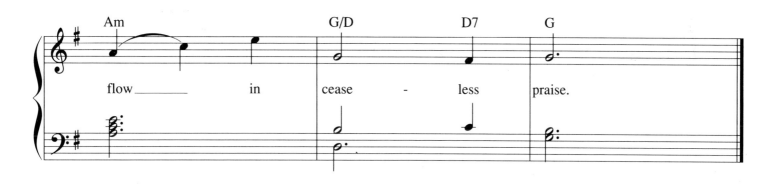

2. Take my hands, and let them move
   At the impulse of Thy love;
   Take my feet, and let them be
   Swift and beautiful for Thee.

3. Take my voice, and let me sing
   Always, only, for my King;
   Take my lips, and let them be
   Filled with messages from thee.

4. Take my silver and my gold,
   Not a mite would I withold;
   Take my intellect, and use
   Every power as Thou shalt choose.

5. Take my will, and make it thine;
   It shall be no longer mine;
   Take my heart - it is Thine own;
   It shall be Thy royal throne.

6. Take my love; my Lord, I pour
   At Thy feet its treasure-store;
   Take myself, and I will be
   Ever, only, all for Thee.

The Lord's My Shepherd

Music: Melody by Jessie S. Irvine (1836-1887)
Words: Francis Rous (1579-1659)

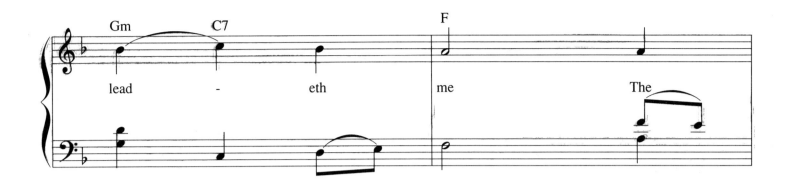

lead - eth me The

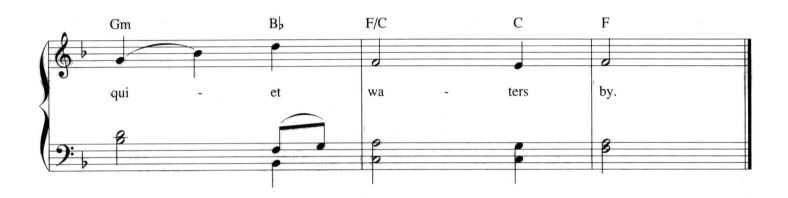

qui - et wa - ters by.

2. My soul He doth restore again,
   And me to walk doth make
   Within the paths of righteousness,
   E'en for His own name's sake.

3. Yea, though I walk in death's dark vale,
   Yet will I fear no ill;
   For Thou art with me, and Thy rod
   And staff me comfort still.

4. My table Thou hast furnished
   In presence of my foes;
   My head Thou dost with oil anoint,
   And my cup overflows.

5. Goodness and mercy all my life
   Shall surely follow me,
   And in God's house for evermore
   My dwelling-place shall be.

Thine Be The Glory

Music: G.F. Handel (1685-1759)
Words: Edmund Budry (1854-1932),
tr. R. Birch Hoyle (1875-1939)

Suggested registration: Brass   Rhythm: Rock

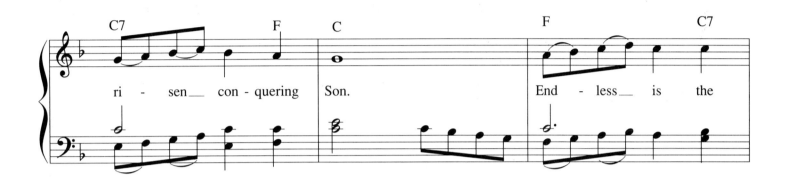

2. Lo, Jesus meets us, risen from the tomb;
    Lovingly He greets us, scatters fear and gloom;
    Let the church with gladness hymns of triumph sing,
    For her Lord now liveth, death hast lost its sting.

Refrain

3. No more we doubt Thee, glorious Prince of Life;
    Life is nought without Thee: aid us in our strife;
    Make us more than conquerers through Thy deathless love;
    Bring us safe through Jordan to Thy home above:

Refrain

Were You There

Music: American Folk Hymn

Suggested registration: Organ   Rhythm: No rhythm

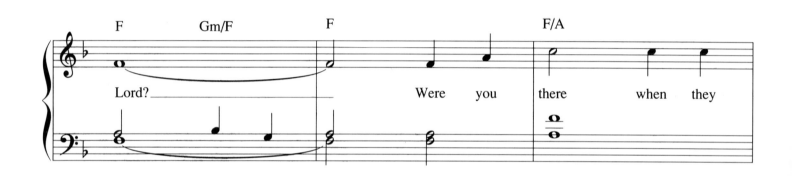

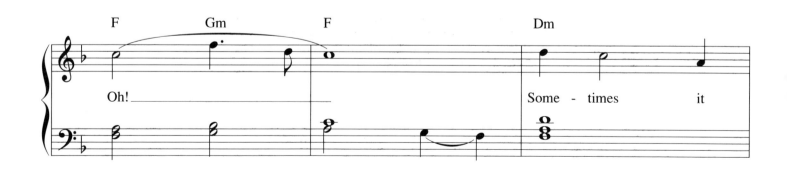

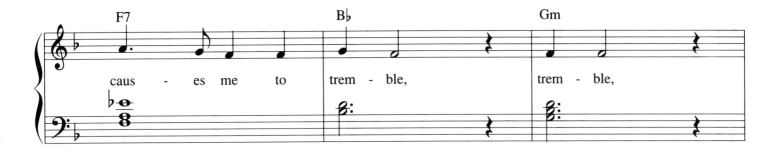

caus - es me to trem - ble, trem - ble,

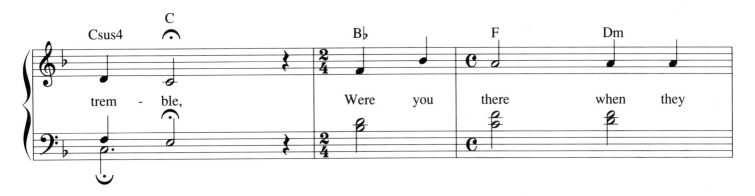

trem - ble, Were you there when they

cru - ci - fied my Lord? _____

2. Were you there when they nailed Him to the tree?
Were you there when they nailed Him to the tree?
Oh! Sometimes it causes me to tremble, tremble, tremble;
Were you there when they nailed Him to the tree?

3. Were you there when they laid Him in the tomb?
Were you there when they laid Him in the tomb?
Oh! Sometimes it causes me to tremble, tremble, tremble;
Were you there when they laid him in the tomb?

4. Were you there when God raised him from the dead?
Were you there when God raised him from the dead?
Oh! Sometimes it causes me to tremble, tremble, tremble;
Were you there when God raised him from the dead?

What A Friend

Music: C. C. Converse (1832-1918)
Words: Joseph Scriven (1819-1886)

Suggested registration: Piano   Rhythm: 8 beat

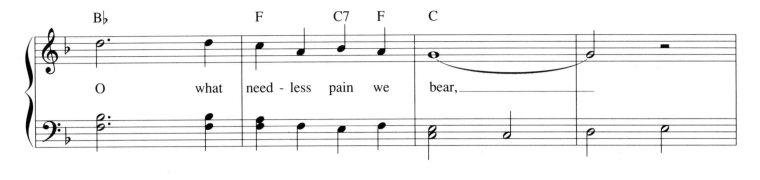

O _ what need-less pain we bear,____

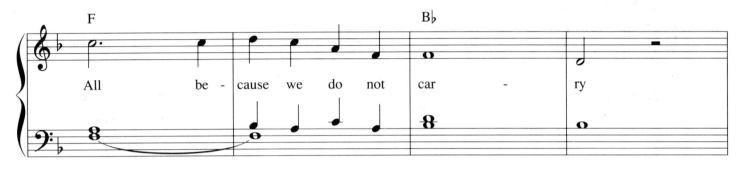

All _ be-cause we do not car - ry

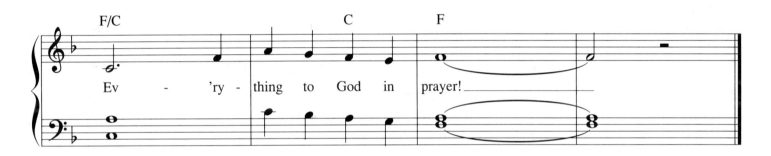

Ev - 'ry - thing to God in prayer!____

2. Have we trials and temptations,
   Is there trouble anywhere?
   We should never be discouraged:
   Take it to the Lord in prayer.
   Can we find a friend so faithful
   Who will all our sorrows share?
   Jesus knows our every weakness;
   Take it to the Lord in prayer.

3. Are we weak and heavy-laden,
   Cumbered with a load of care?
   Precious saviour, still our refuge,
   Take it to the Lord in prayer!
   Do thy friends despise, forsake thee?
   Take it to the Lord in prayer;
   In his arms he'll take and shield thee,
   Thou wilt find a solace there.

When I Survey The Wondrous Cross

Music: E. Miller (1731-1807)
Words: Isaac Watts (1674-1748)

Suggested registration: Organ   Rhythm: Waltz

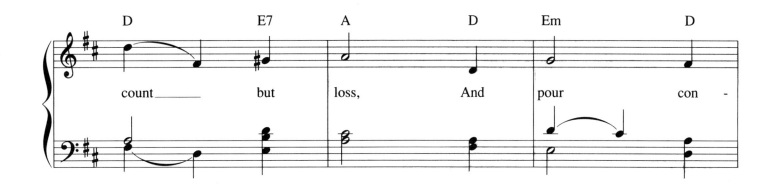

count____ but loss, And pour con -

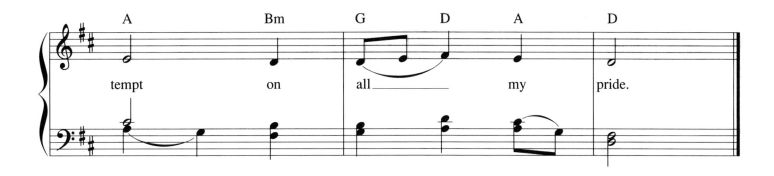

tempt on all____ my pride.

2. Forbid it, Lord, that I should boast
   Save in the death of Christ my God;
   All the vain things that charm me most,
   I sacrifice them to His blood.

3. See from His head, His hands, His feet,
   Sorrow and love flow mingled down;
   Did e'er such love and sorrow meet,
   Or thorns compose so rich a crown?

4. His dying crimson, like a robe,
   Spreads o'er his body on the tree;
   Then am I dead to all the globe,
   And all the globe is dead to me.

5. Were the whole realm of nature mine,
   That were a present far too small;
   Love so amazing, so divine,
   Demands my soul, my life, my all.

Ye Servants Of God

Music: C.H.H. Parry (1848-1918)
Words: Charles Wesley (1707-1788) (altered)

Suggested registration: Organ   Rhythm: Waltz

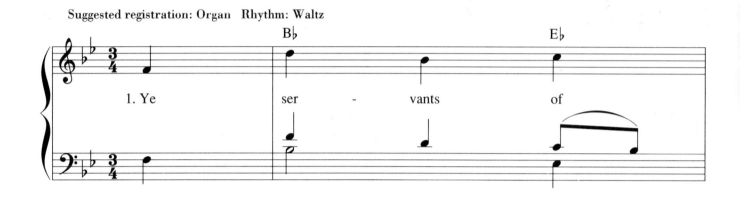

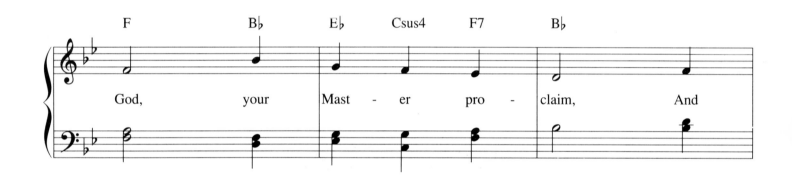

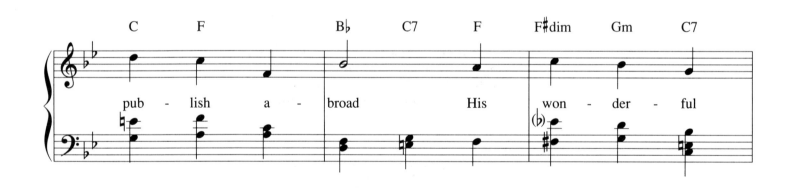

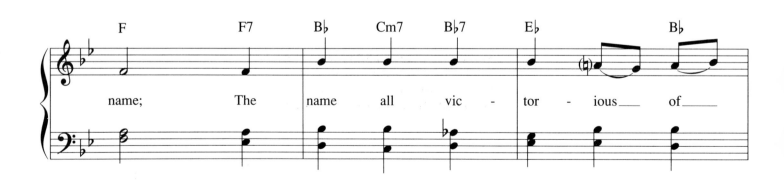

Jes - us ex - tol; His king - dom is

glor - ious, and rules ov - er all.

2. God ruleth on high, almighty to save:
   And still He is nigh, His presence we have;
   The great congregation his triumph shall sing,
   Ascribing salvation to Jesus our King.

3. "Salvation to God who sits on the throne!"
   Let all cry aloud and honour the Son;
   The praises of Jesus the angels proclaim,
   Fall down on their faces, and worship the Lamb.

4. Then let us adore, and give Him His right:
   All glory and power, all wisdom and might,
   All honour and blessing, with angels above,
   And thanks never-ceasing, and infinite love.

The Church's One Foundation

Music: S.S. Wesley (1810-1876)
Words: Samuel John Stone (1839-1900)

Suggested registration: Organ   Rhythm: 8 beat

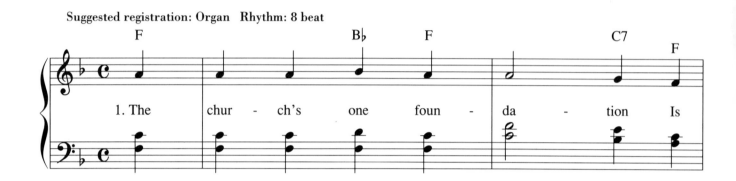

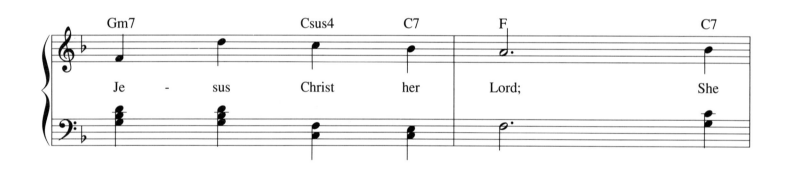

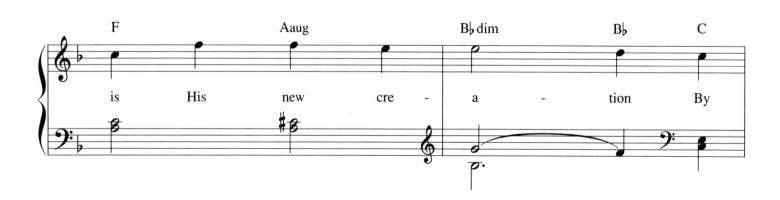

wa - ter and the word; From

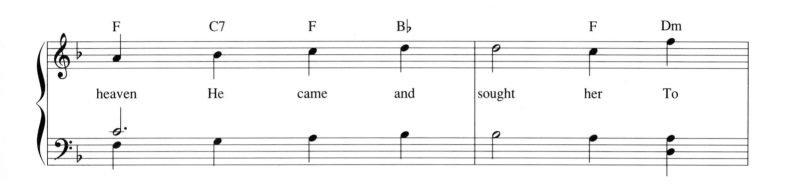

heaven He came and sought her To

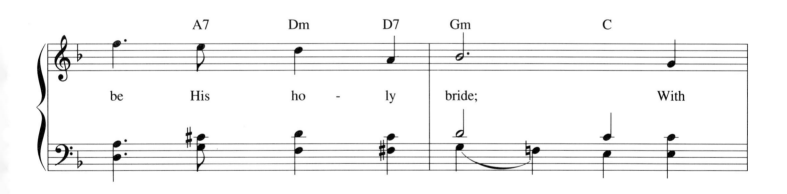

be His ho - ly bride; With

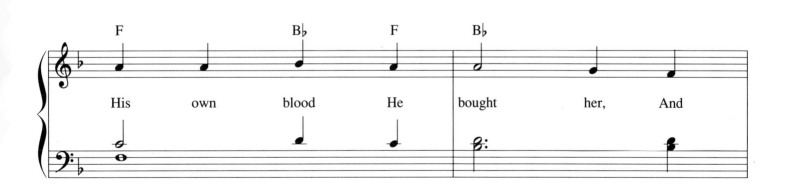

His own blood He bought her, And

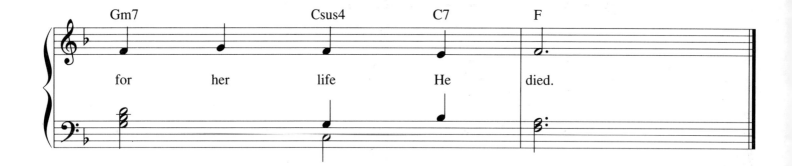

for her life He died.

2. Elect from every nation,
   Yet one o'er all the earth,
   Her charter of salvation
   One Lord, one faith, one birth;
   One holy name she blesses,
   Partakes one holy food,
   And to one hope she presses
   With every grace endued.

3. 'Mid toil and tribulation,
   And tumult of her war,
   She waits the consummation
   Of peace for evermore;
   Till with the vision glorious
   Her longing eyes are blessed,
   And the great church victorious
   Shall be the church at rest.

4. Yet she on earth has union
   With God the Three in One,
   And mystic sweet communion
   With those whose rest is won.
   O happy ones and holy!
   Lord, give us grace that we,
   Like them, the meek and lowly,
   On high may deal with Thee.

Thy Kingdom Come, O God

Music: S.L.G. Hayne (1836-1883)
Words: L. Heasley (1824-1905)

2. Where is Thy reign of peace,
   And purity, and love?
   When shall all hatred cease,
   As in the realms above?

3. When comes the promised time,
   That war shall be no more,
   And lost, oppression, came
   Shall flee Thy face before?

4. We pray Thee, Lord, arise,
   And come in thy great might;
   Revive our longing eyes,
   Which languish for Thy sight.

5. Men scorn thy sacred name,
   And wolves devour Thy fold;
   By many deeds of shame
   We learn that love grows cold.

6. O'er lands both near and far
   Thick darkness broodeth yet:
   Arise, O morning star,
   Arise, and never set!

Swing Low, Sweet Chariot

Music: Spiritual, Traditional